The Only Lesson

Bill McKenna

Phil Nash
Editor

BALBOA.
PRESS
A DIVISION OF HAY HOUSE

Balboa Press books may be ordered through booksellers or by contacting:

Balboa Press
A Division of Hay House
1663 Liberty Drive
Bloomington, IN 47403
www.balboapress.com
1-(877) 407-4847

Because of the dynamic nature of the Internet, any web addresses or links contained in this book may have changed since publication and may no longer be valid. The views expressed in this work are solely those of the author and do not necessarily reflect the views of the publisher, and the publisher hereby disclaims any responsibility for them.

The author of this book does not dispense medical advice or prescribe the use of any technique as a form of treatment for physical, emotional, or medical problems without the advice of a physician, either directly or indirectly. The intent of the author is only to offer information of a general nature to help you in your quest for emotional and spiritual well-being. In the event you use any of the information in this book for yourself, which is your constitutional right, the author and the publisher assume no responsibility for your actions.

Any people depicted in stock imagery provided by Thinkstock are models, and such images are being used for illustrative purposes only.
Certain stock imagery © Thinkstock.

ISBN: 978-1-4525-3502-9 (sc)
ISBN: 978-1-4525-3504-3 (hc)
ISBN: 978-1-4525-3503-6 (e)

Library of Congress Control Number: 2011907615

Printed in the United States of America

Balboa Press rev. date: 6/3/2011

Table of Contents

Dedication

To my wife Michelle, with out you this book would not exist. To Mom, Dad, Kathy, Suzi, Frankie, Mary, Danny, Joanne, Patrick, Bridget, Erin, Sarah and Elizabeth. Thank you for every minute. To Sister Joan Marie Sasse, OSB. Thank you for turning the lights on. To Dr. Masaru Emoto. Thank you for the generous use of your work and your gifts to the world. To Phil Nash, thank you for marrying my sister, the free meals at Tangs and doing the editing. To everyone that I have ever met, thank you. You all have my unconditional love.

Forward

If you have this in your hands right now it's not an accident. It contains the single most important message you will read in your lifetime. If you happen to believe in reincarnation then this message is still the most important for this life and all lifetimes prior.

Quickly look back at the past few days prior to coming in contact with this book. How did it happen? Were you delayed, walked in a bookstore and it caught your eye? Was it a gift? Did you just randomly pull it off your friend's book shelf? What were all the events that led up to it? If you pause to reflect, many subtle seemingly unconnected events put this book in your hands. This is not a coincidence.

It is my sincere hope that all of the events that brought you to this book make perfect sense to you by the time you complete it.

My perception of my family life is just that. My perception. It was necessary to disclose it to you in order for you the reader to be able to make sense of everything. I am one of 12 children and each one had a different experience and perception. Some names or events have been altered to protect others, but everything you read here is the truth.

"These interrogation/endurance sessions...instilled a great amount of fear in me and that fear propelled me in many ways throughout my life."

"I avoided like the plague people who I perceived had done me wrong - lied, cheated, stole or just berated me with judgemental foul remarks."

Chapter 1: Youth

My earliest memories are very happy. I remember waking up in my bed, running down the hall, so excited to see my father and to jump into his bed for another bout of wrestling. We wrestle, play and laugh. It is so much fun. I am probably not yet two years old. Then I decide to bite him. Wow! That got a reaction. I received the first beating of my life. No more wrestling bouts. I thought I bit him on the leg, but reflecting on his reaction from the perspective of a "grown-ass man" to quote Oprah, I'm going to guess I took a bite out of his manhood.

I was born in the early Sixties to a second-generation Irish couple. My grandparents on both sides fled the hardships of Ireland for opportunities in America. They settled in New York City where my parents met and were married before they moved to Chula Vista, California. We lived a few miles from the Mexican border in the most southwest part of the United States. I was the third oldest of 12 children and the oldest boy in our strict Irish-Catholic family.

I recall being terribly angry as a child and this carried into my adulthood. I was prone to fits of rage. I had a terrible temper which I just could not control. I do remember a brief period at the very beginning of my life - my earliest happy memories of running down the hall to wrestle with my father. Then came the bite and its aftermath. Not long after that I walked in on my father beating up my mother. I was enraged and frightened. I stood in between them and screamed at him "don't hit my mom!" I was quickly ushered out and sent to my room. I can still recall how it felt.

"When I get bigger, I'm going to beat him up."

I desperately wanted him to die. I lived in fear of him and what might erupt at any moment. His anger was intense and unbridled. He disciplined through violence and the threat of it, coupled with techniques that seemed to come straight from the interrogation operation manuals of the CIA, KGB and Seal Team

One. He would use a delightful combination of sleep deprivation, repetition, anger and threats sprinkled in with an assortment of well-timed and unexplained slaps, punches and choking. He walloped with belts or other handy tools of the trade at hand as he vacillated between being good cop/bad cop. These interrogation/endurance sessions would go from days at a time stretching out to months in a few cases. They instilled a great amount of fear in me and that fear propelled me in many ways throughout my life. Fear manifested itself as generalized anger, hate, jealousy, judgement, violence, racism and assorted insecurities. On the flip side, I developed mental and physical endurance, focus as well as a high pain threshold.

I left home when I was 18, not a particularly big deal for me because I had been working since I could remember. My wife loves the story of my very first job. At three years old I would get on my tricycle and go knocking door to door asking, "You got any cookies?" I was pretty successful at it, going farther and farther until I was all the way around the corner on the other block. It was far enough away for people not to know who I belonged to, a long distance in those days. It's a wonder I was never harmed or worse. I always chalked that up to others instinctively knowing that "this one here is just too surly, I will certainly get bit in the process." I learned early in life that if you got out of the house before Dad got out of bed you had much better odds of not being the focus of a beating or an endurance session.

A child was born in our house every 18 months from the time I was five to 18 years old. Both my parents worked, so the older kids looked after the younger ones, cooked the meals and had, how shall I say it, "a liability exposure," for a beating should anything go wrong, as it often did. This was cause for concern and I was none too happy about the job. As you can imagine, there was also quite a bit of thrashing between the siblings, with lots of humor thrown in strangely enough.

Every kid in the house was "given" a song, usually about someone in their class that we perceived that they liked. All the kids would gang up and sing it to the targeted sibling of the moment/hour/day as they screamed and cried. This was inevitably followed by another family favorite song we made up called "feeling sorry for yourself," which was nothing more than those words melodically sung over and over. Somehow it gave us all great comfort, or at least those of us who were not the target of the moment.

I discovered an interest in martial arts from the age of eight. I desperately wanted to go to a local karate school but that was vetoed by parents who already considered me too violent. The last thing they needed was for me to become skilled at my propensity for opening up a can of whoop ass. The desire to learn martial arts was very strong. I convinced other students to teach me. I read books, learned about every pressure point I could and even organized lessons in the garage from other teachers before I was old enough to get a job and peddle to schools myself. I studied about 18 different styles earning a variety of color belts before getting my black belt at the age of 20.

Where we grew up and went to high school the whites were the overwhelming minority. My classmates were primarily Mexican, Filipino and Black. Chula Vista and Imperial Beach were essentially low income, border towns. Surrounded by other cultures, as a white, Irish-American kid I experienced what many minorities do. Having anger issues and a large chip on my shoulder sure did not make matters any better.

I reflected back the prejudices and violence that I experienced, becoming just as prejudiced. As a child, it was all I knew. I thought to myself "this is just how life is and everyone is going to either try to give you a beating or take something from you."

I adopted my own ways of dealing with life. At 14 I bought a bike and foul weather gear, which gave me the freedom to get a better job (cookie begging only takes you so far as you get older). The bike also equaled self-reliance. I didn't have to beg friends for rides every day to get back and forth to school which was about 20 miles away. Why so far away? I went to high school about two miles from the border, a private Catholic school. I was told "you are going there, and by the way you are paying for it too." Working late at night kept me off the "radar" and put cash in my pocket, which to me meant more independence. By the time I was 18 I had already put nearly 13,000 miles on my bike. I had a little odometer that I was so proud of.

I left the house at 18 for college. My college years were great. I felt in-the-moment and proud that I was accomplishing something. Yet I still felt a deep-seated anger. I had no idea what my anger was about but I knew it was there. I was enjoying that period of my life and having fun, but would often run into hostile people. I chalked this up to reality, reinforcing my early established beliefs.

I found conflict everywhere. I came to the conclusion that jerks were just omnipresent. I would swear on a stack of bibles that I was being discriminated against because there was no logical reason for people to treat me the way I was being treated. I did not say a word to anybody and yet they gave me the "stink eye." I was in the right and "they" were the jerks. I wanted every one of color or minorities to feel what this white guy was feeling, so they could see it was happening to everyone, or so I thought.

I avoided like the plague people who I perceived had done me wrong - lied, cheated, stole or just berated me with judgemental foul remarks. If you don't let anything go, that is quite the dance to do. It ends up being a pretty long list of people to avoid.

After getting my degree, I worked a regular job for the next 25-plus years. I was angry about the past and fearful of the future. I kind of felt like a jerk, did not like myself all that much other than the very brief moment when a goal was accomplished.

After college through my 20's, 30's and early 40's my life continued to be filled with what many would consider intense experiences. Shortly after earning my black belt, I started running endurance races, eventually completing the Western States 100, which as the name implies, is a 100 mile race along a trail in the Sierra Nevada mountains that goes from snow to 114 degrees. I became passionate about sky diving and performed many jumps, before almost dying on St. Patrick's Day when my chute collapsed hundreds of feet above the ground. I learned to fly airplanes and helicopters, eventually buying a few helicopters of my own. I bought and lived on a yacht in Mexico. I experienced both financial success, becoming a multi-millionaire, and financial catastrophe a few times over. I struggled through crash-and-burn relationships and struggled with depression. None of these life experiences compared to the intensity of what I was about to experience, all of it quite by accident, and as my sister said, to the unlikeliest of people.

"Mayday, mayday, mayday. This
is the vessel Sea Hunt 20 miles
south of Ensenada. We hit a rock
and are taking on water."

_____

"I wanted to put my dream down, literally,
on the bottom of the ocean floor."

Chapter 2: Yacht

I began dreaming of owning a yacht around the age of five. I fantasized that I would get one as large as a cruise ship for my birthday. I'm not sure what I would have done with a ship that size at that age but "a girls gotta have dreams" you know. Several years ago my dream came true when I purchased a yacht. Although not exactly cruise ship size, I loved it and enjoyed countless days and nights aboard.

During my first summer with the yacht I visited Avalon, the small harbor city on Catalina Island 26 miles across the sea from Southern California. Fast asleep one night while moored in the harbor, I had the most vivid dream of my life. I was aboard the yacht and at the helm in the pilot house on a pitch black night. Suddenly a huge rock cliff, part of an island, appeared on the left side of the boat. We hit the rock cliff. I was thrown forward into the helm and the entire vessel listed to the right. Shock and horror filled me. I heard scrapping and tearing as the rock tore into the left side of the boat. I woke from this dream in a sweat, my heart pounding because it all seemed so real. I was grateful it was not.

A year passed and I found myself traveling north up the coast of Mexico, headed to Catalina Island for some serious rest and relaxation. Aboard was a Mexican national serving as a deck hand named Miguel. Also on board was Richard, a wealthy retired guy from the USA whom I had met in Puerto Vallarta. Richard had spent a lot of time at sea and though I did not know him that well, I was happy to have his help on-board. I knew that I needed more than just Miguel and me for the trip north.

Richard was an investment banker who had done well for himself and retired early. Initially he seemed fine, with entertaining stories, but when he talked about his work as an investment banker I became a little uneasy. For example, when he found conflict he loved to sue. If he lost a case, he didn't take it well. He described hiring a private eye to dig up dirt about his legal adversary, uncovering an affair and sending pictures to the perpetrator's wife. There were more stories like that, and he seemed almost proud of his paybacks. My uneasiness wasn't helped by the small quarters of the ship, but I tried to steer the conversation to the positive stuff. My plan was to drop off the Miguel in Ensenada just before the U.S. border, stop in San Diego just long enough to refuel, get a new pair of running shoes, drop off Richard and then off to Catalina to recreate the best summer of my life. I was all about keeping things positive.

Just south of Ensenada I was at the helm while the others slept. I noticed three numbers that appear to me occasionally, usually as reassurance about accomplishing a goal. The number combination "308" was everywhere, appearing on all the different systems. I thought "that's cool, going to the island and the universe is saying way to go! Right on course!" I had never seen it displayed to me so much. At the same time, I began to have this very uneasy feeling that something was wrong. I attempted to scale down on the computerized radar screen and it locked up completely. I did not want to reboot the computer because I would then lose my other navigation system. The system showed us several miles from some small islands off coast, but I was concerned about other ships so I went to our second radar system and scaled that down. We looked good other than the very center of the display which usually has a little clutter. I was still uneasy. I tried to look outside but it was absolutely pitch black. I sat back down at the helm and then it happened... a long scratching and crunching sound as a huge rock cliff appeared to my left. I was thrown forward into the helm as we rolled over to the right. I was not even sure if this was real because it was happening just as I dreamt it in every detail. I could hear Miguel in the forward bunk cussing up a storm in Spanish and somehow for just a flash his cussing struck me as hilarious. Terror and chaos ensued. The smell of wood and fiberglass filled my nose as I checked on the crew. Every one okay? Yes. I ran to the engine room. No water there, so I dogged down the hatch. The crew reported that we were taking on water in the forward. I had to move away from the island so a wave did not come and smash us to bits. It was still pitch black. I could not see what we hit or tell where we were. I zoomed in on the electronic map and navigated backwards on the same track that I crashed into the island on. A few minutes later we were back at open sea.

"Mayday, mayday, mayday. This is the vessel Sea Hunt 20 miles south of Ensenada. We hit a rock and are taking on water."

Silence. Not the good kind. "Mayday, mayday mayday....." Finally, a scratchy and garbled reply comes back.

"This is the United States Coast Guard Station San Diego. Are you in immediate danger?"

"I think so, we are taking on water."

"Okay, we'll launch the helicopter."

I radioed back for the coast guard to stand down while I looked to see how bad it was. It's 11:45 pm. I went forward and it was torn up. We had water but were not sinking. I recalled an old movie about John F. Kennedy and his boat PT-109 during World War II. He had taken a hit below the water line and he throttled down to lift the front of the boat out of the water. If it worked for JFK, I decided to try it too. Miguel went forward to send back word how it was going. I throttled down and it actually forced a ton of water in. It was coming in very fast. Miguel was cussing again. I backed off the throttle. Even at that point my mind raced forward. Out of imminent danger, I didn't want to go through what I knew would happen next - insurance companies, shipyards, conflict over repairs. I knew it would take many months, perhaps over a year to repair and who knew if even then it would be right. I was deflated and depressed. I wanted to put my dream down, literally, on the bottom of the ocean floor. I could do it too, just by hitting the throttle. In minutes the ship would be on the bottom and we'd be safe in a coast guard helicopter or boat. I desperately wanted to do it but also knew that if I did it deliberately, Richard would eventually get me. So we limped into Ensenada, put a patch on and about a week later headed to a shipyard in San Diego to begin the long painful process of bringing the yacht back to her pre-wreck condition. It was just as painful as I thought it would be, filled with conflict of all kinds from all directions.

The next day, as I sat eating a street taco I had a strong feeling that the accident was for a reason, like being forced to stop so something could happen. I looked around and did not notice anything. Surely, the wreck didn't happen so I can enjoy a delicious taco, although I can't seem to get enough of them in my diet. Months passed as the repairs dragged on. A summer in a ship yard is not so fun. I continued to feel that same premonition but never saw anything that remotely looked like a good reason for a yacht wreck!

———————

"I began to see that if I just could understand what it meant to be an intuitive, we would have a much better chance of making it."

———————

Chapter 3: Michelle

On a guy's night out during the months my boat was being repaired, I ran into my old girlfriend Michelle. Alright, I'll admit it I did not run into her, I called her. I missed her. I loved her but we just could not seem to get along very well. We had been in an on-and-off relationship for years and I had known her most of my life. In high school, her locker was just below mine. She likes to tell people that I used to look at her "all creepy like." I freely admit that I did and still do! I always liked her. We had several go-arounds in our 20's and 30's. I considered her my soul mate but for some reason we could not get it together. I found her incredibly unreasonable and she would often resist a decision I made for what appeared to be no logical reason. I could not understand her unwillingness to be around certain people or to go to a certain place on a certain day. She was often in pain. Headaches and stomach aches occurred multiple times per day. I just could not understand why.

Now in my 40's I decided to give it one last try. I was committed to doing whatever I had to do to understand her better and to enhance our communications so we could move on to getting married and starting a family. She was always very sensitive and seemed to be an incredibly good guesser. Little by little I came to know just how good she was. We started to play games.

"What number am I thinking of between 1 and 100?"

It was 72 and yes she got it right! Shocked but considering myself very logical I thought it was just luck. I started asking her just to tell me what mental picture was in my mind.

"Ah...let's see...ah, ok. It's a fruit...Ahh...lime, no...it's a lemon".

"Damm!!! What? No way. No possible way."

One morning aboard the yacht the low battery alarm went off at 4 a.m. while we were fast asleep below. Damm it! I got out of bed, turn on the generator to recharge things and go back to bed. Usually the batteries last well into the next day. I awaken hours later and spend the day trying to figure out why the batteries are running low. Everything seems to be working normally. The next morning beeeeep beeeeeep beeeeeep beeeep, it's 4 a.m. Ahhhhh. I jump out of bed to go start the generator. Now I am mad and I cannot sleep. I open some of covers to look at the wires behind. I don't know what I am doing as I look into this large nest of wires that combined are about the thickness of two telephone poles. How am I going to find the problem? I am going to have to fly someone in and it's going to cost a fortune. Plus I won't be able to sleep until I take care of this.

A few hours later Michelle gets up and can see I am very frustrated. She walks over to the electric panel and puts her hand over it. She moves her hand around and delivers her diagnosis.

"It's in the galley (kitchen). Um, the refrigerator. Ah no, it's the freezer."

Okay. I go look in the freezer and find it completely frosted over inside. I go to the panel and turn off the power to the freezer and as I do, the electric demand gauge drops down to next to nothing. It turns out that the frost creates resistance and demands more power. Problem solved. I could not believe it. I called a close friend named Chris and told him about it. Chris happens to be an electrical engineer who works on all kinds of very high tech stuff for the military. He is very logical like myself. We were both astounded.

That weekend the phone rings at 8 p.m. It's Chris. He is working on a 1960's Mustang. The car will not keep a charge and won't start. He and another electrical engineer get together in the garage at night to have a beer and work on the Mustang for fun. After several random Friday nights trying to figure the problem out the fun is turning into frustration. Chris laughingly asks to talk to Michelle thanks to her success solving the power issue on the yacht. He explains his theory that the issue is between the alternator and/or a wire to it. Is it this color wire or that? She stops him, "Chris, does it have a new radio?"

"Yes, Michelle, but that's not the issue. Just tell me your thoughts on the alternator."

"Okay, Chris what I want you to do is pull the power to the radio."

"Sure."

Click. The conversation is over. An hour passes, I call Chris back.

"Hey, Chris did you pull the power to the radio?"

"No, I think it is in the ignition and I have these three wires in my hand, can you ask her to tell me which color one..."

"Chris," pipes in Michelle, "just pull the power to the radio!" A few muffled cuss words on the other end, and then "Okay, I'll do it!" The phone gets put down as we can hear rustling in the background, a grunt and then screams followed by the sound of an engine start. Chris did not know what to say. He was so freaked out I did not hear from him for a month.

How the heck can she do that? Well, as it turns out she is intuitive, clairvoyant and empathic. I initially did not put much thought into how this impacted our relationship. Over time I began to notice that she had this gift but could not turn it off. It was such a large part of who she was day in and day out. I began to see that if I just could understand what it meant to be an intuitive, we would have a much better chance of making it. I purchased about 15 books on developing intuition, clairvoyance, clairsentience, clairaudience and communications with angels/spiritual guides. I started reading. The first thing I found out was that it is common for intuitives who receive their information though physical sensation to get headaches, stomach aches and other pains when they encountered someone who is angry or experiencing negative feelings. I dropped the book and ran to her, more excited than a four year old on Christmas morning seeing the presents and tree.

"Honey, honey, honey, I got it. The aches are related to you being intuitive."

She was a bit doubtful but agreed to try an experiment. We agreed to walk around town, go to the grocery store and visit a few places where I knew we could find a few of what I like to call "hostiles." The results were remarkable. Every time we encountered a hostile she would buckle over in pain or get a severe headache. The test went on for a few months with me giving her a literal "gut check" everywhere we went.

It was amazing to see how many people are living in an angry hostile state. Michelle's past actions started to make more sense to me. I recalled an instance where she would not go with me to my friend's house. I remembered thinking that I have known these people for a long time. I hang out with the husband but not so much my friend's wife. They are good people. I saw no good reason for my wife unwillingness to hang out with this couple.

"So what the heck is the problem? Is Michelle just being mean for no good reason?"

After our hostile experiment, it all became clear. The wife of my friend was harboring some ill feelings towards me, but I just could not see it through the smiles and pleasantries. Michelle opened my eyes to how my friend's wife was really feeling. As I mentally reviewed the events of the past everything made sense, but most of all Michelle's actions made so much more sense to me. We were both learning.

Main new concepts I learned:

- An entire world exists beyond the physical logical world.
- Some people can access information from this dimension.
- Other people's thoughts or feelings can be felt by an empathic.

"It's like drinking poison and expecting the other person to get sick."

————————————

"I finally figured out that forgiveness is the key to the handcuffs that bind us to the people who did us wrong. If we never put the key in the locked cuffs we are stuck with the other person for life.

Chapter 4 : Aw Heck, I'll Do It: Learning to Forgive

I kept reading five, six, seven and more books… and by the 11th I started to notice a recurring theme. It goes something like this… all humans have spiritual guides or angels. You can communicate and get information and guidance from the higher realm. Angels or Divine Guides dwell in what they call a higher frequency and in order to receive a connection, guidance and/or information from them, you need to let go of what they call "low frequency thoughts" like anger, resentment, revenge and ill feelings. In short you have to forgive. Through the action of forgiving, you raise up to a higher frequency and level of communication.

"Well heck now, you know letting people off the hook was never one of my strong suits."

When it came to forgiving, I'd break before I'd bend. I had always felt that if I forgave someone, I was condoning the behavior that needed forgiving or that I would then have to spend time with the person. Now I know neither is true. I had held on to being unforgiving - and all that went along with it - with a vice-like grip for my entire life. It took a while to digest this revelation. Could it really be true that I could get all this type of information that my wife receives if I just forgive? Who would I be if I left all that anger behind? My resentments kept me safe. Although I had not given it that much thought, my feeling was that by holding onto my anger and resentment, somehow the other person would be punished. In reality, the other person is unaffected. The anger just causes me to re-live the offense, not to mention the ill feelings, over and over again. This resulted in all kinds of negative experiences and brought to mind that saying, "it's like drinking poison and expecting the other person to get sick." It just never occurred to me that drinking poison was exactly what I was doing.

On one side of my mental scale I weighed what I received by holding on to my feelings of being victimized. On the other side I looked at the potential benefit of getting divine guidance. I thought to myself, are you going to get a new car, house, money in your pocket or anything, anything at all from holding on to the resentment? The answer came back, no, no and no again. I asked myself if my resentment had truly caused the people who had wronged me to suffer and were they suffering right now? The answer came back that any suffering they had was very minimal and they were really not suffering now. In most cases they did not suffer at all and seemed almost oblivious to what they had done. From that perspective the decision to forgive and let go seemed easy. I reasoned that I was not really getting much out of holding on to the hostility yet the potential gain from letting go would quite literally be out of this world. I saw first-hand evidence that the spiritually-connected information my wife was receiving was correct and coming in hour by hour, all day every day. I decided to do it.

I had no idea how that one act would set me on a course to the unimaginable.

The first and overwhelmingly significant forgiveness was towards my father. I did it without telling him. I just let it all go. I felt lighter but at the same time it felt like a piece of me was missing. It is a weird feeling when you have carried around something for your entire life and then it's gone. I recalled the things he had done and sacrificed to help me. I started to become grateful. He was a man with his own set of struggles who had taken on a tremendous amount of responsibility for anyone to handle.

Looking back, the way I built a wall between my father and me is both funny and sad. For years, I did not go to events where I knew he was going to be. When I gave in and went to an event where he was, he would follow me around while I tried to distance myself. I have 11 siblings, with a full complement of spouses and kids, so it's quite the big crowd when we get together. At these events, my dad and I were doing our own strange dance.

I would constantly come up with strategies for my next steps. You always have an exit strategy. If he moves into the room, you go to the next. Keep people in between the two of you. It was a real circus because he was always looking to get at me and I was always moving away. There were a lot of sudden exits on my part from family get-togethers, but everyone in the family knew the deal.

Months after forgiving my father I went to a family event and my father was there. I gave him a hug and I did not avoid him. A few hours into the party I was in a tight hallway and my father approached to tell a story about a guy who was smoking a cigar in his office. My father told him to get out. Since the man has the cigar in his teeth, when my father pressed his belly into him, the lit end of the man's cigar was smashed into my father's face. My father is about two inches from my face acting out the story and I am being sprayed with spit. He did not have what you might call fresh breath. I can tell he is really just mad at me and this story is an excuse to express this anger. I just stayed there for him. I felt nothing but compassion for him. I did not have any of the "get the hell out of here" emotions that dominated my life prior. I let him finish his story, after which he calmed down and backed away. The party went on and I did nothing to avoid him but he did not approach. Months later I heard from my sister who talked to him. He told her "you know Billy has changed." In all subsequent family events it was as if I almost did not exist. He lost all focus where I was concerned. I was now just another member of the family.

Other situations started to present themselves to me, I spent a summer prior to all of these changes aboard the yacht back in Avalon harbor off Catalina Island. Avalon is small town. I believed in frequenting the locally owned, full-price (and them some) organic grocery/marine store, using it instead of the chain store to help support the locals. I spent thousands of dollars in this small store. Late that summer I visited the store for some grapes among other things. As I laid them on the counter for the owner to ring up, the grapes looked so good that without thinking about what I was doing, I picked a grape off the bundle and popped it in my mouth. Before I got the first chew down, the "known hostile" owner who was ringing me up, irately said, "You know that is stealing. You cannot eat the grapes before I ring them up." Whew, now that just lit my fuse. I paid the bill and walked out. When I returned to the yacht I was still screaming mad. How dare she? I'm not like that. I don't steal. I returned to the store and laid a $20.00 bill on the counter, telling the owners that this was to pay for the grapes. She said "no, no, that is too much" I said no, I want to make sure that you get your full due and no one is thinking I am stealing anything. I left the $20.00, walked out and did not go back the rest of the summer. I avoided her in town and that is not easy in a place that is literally one square mile. We started calling her "Grape-Nut" behind her back. It was funny to us but I was angry at her and would not let it go.

Summer turned to fall and we left the island. The next year we migrated back to Avalon. A lot had changed for me but I still had a very important lesson to learn, part of a bigger lesson that Grape-Nut was here to help me with. I got to the island and was very happy. I visited a few friends and was walking about town. I had completely forgotten about Grape-Nut. I turned a corner and there was the old shop. Instinctively I turned around. "Oops, don't go down that street" described my initial reaction and thought process. After about a week of this, it hit me. I needed to forgive her too. I did it right then and there. A few days later I went in and bought some stuff. It felt good. I was free. The gift of forgiveness was for myself although previously I did not want to forgive because I perceived it as a gift for the other person.

Much like the wall shielding me from my father, I had created a prison for myself in the middle of paradise. In fact, over my entire life I had walled myself in.

"Do not go in that mall because you may see you-know-who."

"Don't go down that street because that girl lives there."

"I will never eat at that restaurant again because they did blah blah and I told them I am never coming back, etc., etc., etc."

Actually I have a lot of etceteras on this one because I had been avoiding and resenting for a long time. My resentment or my ego was in control, not me. A good friend and I even came up with our special words for it over three decades back. We would call it "getting tortured" when we would see someone from our past that we held some bad feelings towards and somehow could not avoid them. The funny thing is that neither of us realized to what extent we were really getting tortured. All of these resentments emotionally handcuffed us to the other person.

If we thought of them or ran into them we would get emotionally shanked. My buddy and I could not comprehend that we were shanking ourselves. I finally figured out that forgiveness is the key to the handcuffs that bind us to the people who did us wrong. If we never put the key in the locked cuffs we are stuck with the other person for life.

The fortress that I had built around myself and heart as a method of protection was laid up with the stones of fear in all it's disguises and mortar of retained resentments. The irony is that what I thought was a fortress was nothing but a prison. I built it for myself and was given a self-imposed life term.

Forgiving others also made me consider the odd and twisted benefits people had given to me over the course of my life, and how those gifts had changed my life path. Slowly I started to get it. People I thought had wronged me had something to teach me and were here to help redirect my life path. I had always felt certain people had caused the great tragedies and injustices of my life. Life's rear view mirror now showed it differently, showed it all making perfect sense. Not only did it become easier to completely forgive and let go, but I became grateful for these people and the lessons they taught me. They all helped me to discover the only lesson we are here to learn.

Main new concepts I learned:

- A major block to accessing intuition is not forgiving.
- I get no real life benefits from retained resentments.
- I can forgive and not condone.
- I am punished when I do not forgive, not the person that needs forgiving.
- Forgiveness is a gift for me.
- My resentments handcuffed me to the very people I did not want to be connected to.
- Resentments shrink our world and create a prison for us.
- When I forgive it changes me and the other person.
- When I forgive I become free to go where I want when I want.
- The people that I needed to forgive were here to help and teach me.

———————————

"As I went down my list, forgiving
one person after another, things
started to get weird, real weird. I
asked for and started receiving
guidance and intuitive information."

———————————

Chapter 5: Intuition: A Gift of Forgiving

Prior to my journey of forgiving, intuition was quite foreign to me. I had the random incident as a child of touching my father's car door, instantly hearing myself say, "We are going to get into an accident" and 20 minutes later, whammo, an accident. Another time I saw a motorcycle on the freeway and I thought, "that one is going down" as he passed. Five minutes later traffic slows and starts swerving around. Guess who is face down at the side of the road with motorcycle wheels still spinning? Then there's my previously mentioned and so vivid dream of wrecking the yacht, predicting what actually happened a year later in every exact detail. My wife nicknamed me the "decade psychic" because one intuitive incident seemed to happen to me every ten years. (Yes, she is my full-time heckler and I find it funny).

As I went down my list, forgiving one person after another, things started to get weird, real weird. I asked for and started receiving guidance and intuitive information. I was no longer just the decade psychic. It began with small things. I was absolutely shocked when the information I received was correct. I asked "where is the parking place," as I pulled into a busy shopping mall during the Christmas season. Usually I would just drive around in circles and get frustrated. This time I asked and immediately saw in my mind's eye a space two levels up, left side, three spaces from the end. I drove up the two levels and there it was - three from the end, left side, OPEN! I was just shocked. I said thank you and was still in disbelief.

I then tried asking what the next person coming around the corner was wearing, a little game I made up just for fun. I did not always get it right but it was pretty shocking to see a guy in a red collar short-sleeve shirt walk around the corner or a woman in a flower pattern yellow dress turn the corner when I had just pictured it in my mind moments before. The games were pretty fun and yielded some real world benefits.

"Is this person available for my call right now?"

"Where can I reach this person?"

"Is it better to do this or that right now?"

"Who is the most receptive to what I am selling, Sam or John?"

"What is this guy's real hidden objection?"

As the answers became more consistently correct, it started to make my life easier. So easy, as a matter a fact, that my usual 40/50-hour work week in sales turned into a four-hour work week while my results were the best I had in more than 25 years on the job.

I asked to have a closer and clearer connection with the guides and the divine. I noticed some very strange things starting to happen to me. My wife lost my $28,000 solid gold Rolex watch. She was wearing it because at this point I really did not care about it anymore, it had somehow lost its value to me. She was having a fit for a week but keeping it to herself. She came to me crying, "I lost your watch! I am so sorry." It is hard for her to be intuitive or find things when she gets worried or under pressure. "Honey, I don't care. It's no big deal and if it's gone it's for a reason." My attempts to sooth did not work. I could see the stress had overtaken her. We were aboard the yacht at the time. I really felt absolutely no emotion about it but seeing her distress I closed my eyes and asked, "show me where the watch is." Instantly I saw a golden line appear shooting down through the yacht and then another appeared horizontally. They intersected on her side of the bed. I went downstairs and looked on her side of the bed. Hmmm, nothing except a box of tissues. Maybe it's in the drawer just below. Hmmm, nothing in there. Then I stuck my hand into the box of tissues and there it was.

Things continued to get weird. I was supposed to meet some friends for a four-wheel trip to the desert. We were to rendezvous at a hangar at a small regional airport to pick up several military-style vehicles. Of course I left without taking any directions, but decided to "wing it" in more ways than one. As I neared the airport, I decided, just for fun, to invite one of my spiritual guides to have a seat in the passenger seat next to me. Being pretty new to all this, I still was not sure if these guides were real or my overactive imagination. Nonetheless I asked my guide to point out which way to go. She pointed straight ahead. As I passed a small street that looked to me like it would either dead-end or just continue in a loop back to the road, my guide pointed for me to make a right turn. I reasoned I was imagining all of this because my guide's directions could not be right, and I ignored her. When I passed the street without turning, immediately both her arms went up in the air as if to say, "What the heck? I just showed you what to do and you are not following my guidance."

As I continued to drive, the road took me further away from the airport, so I made a u-turn. Again we neared the point where I had ignored her advice and again she pointed in the same direction as before. "Why not?" I thought to myself as followed her advice, "left, right, and left again." I blindly followed the directions right to the hangar's front door. I was shocked again.

I began to notice people calling me or showing up soon after I thought about them. I began to predict exactly what talk radio hosts were going to say. In big and small ways, the intuitive aspect of my life continued as a gift of forgiving.

Main new concepts I learned:

- Forgiving does help my intuitive abilities.
- Intuition can be called upon at will, it does not have to be a random occurrence.
- Intuition can help in everyday practical matters.
- Information from spiritual guides or intuition is illogical most of the time.

"Suddenly the worry was gone, and with no good reason from the perspective of how I used to look at my life."

————————————

"Yet the best times in my life have come when I was living fully in the moment, not in the past or future."

Chapter 6: I'm So Drunk: More Gifts of Forgiving

The gifts received as a result of forgiving continued taking me in dramatic directions. I read that you can enhance your spiritual connection by taking your energy and focusing it up and out the top of your head. While I have calmed myself down from my long-distance running and skydiving days, I was not about to pass up this opportunity. While I meditated I pulled all my energy from my feet right up my body and out the top of my head. The energy felt so good, it was as if I had entered into the realm of the angels. It felt so light. I remember looking around and saying "gosh you guys up here are so very light and I am so heavy." Although the experience was pure bliss for a few moments, I was a little freaked out so I came right back. The experience stayed with me though.

Over the next few months more strange things started to happen. The upper half of my head felt like there was a lot of energy surrounding it. I felt drunk all day, as if I'd downed a six-pack of beers but remained fully functional. It felt euphoric. At some points it reminded me of being on morphine when I was laid up on the hospital after my sky diving accident. I remember thinking that I would definitely be going to jail if I was pulled over and had drunk enough to feel this good. The top of my head also felt as if someone was very lightly touching my hair or wind was moving it around. I started feeling a more defined area of energy in the form of a circle on the top of my head. This line of energy circled my head where you might wear a baseball cap. It actually felt like I was wearing a cap, maybe a bit too snug, along that line. I found myself crying a lot, but not out of sadness. I cried for no reason, just out of joy.

I began to feel very different than I had ever felt in my life. I was always a worrier, stressed and intense. Suddenly the worry was gone, and with no good reason from the perspective of how I used to look at my life. The worry and stress of everything big and small went away. Everything just started to make sense. Everything just fit together, absolutely perfectly.

The traffic jam that in the past would frustrate me, I now saw that it was setting me up to be in the right place and the right time, and this happened over and over. From the large thing to the very small, everything fit together so perfectly.

The synchronicities of life seemed to suddenly reveal themselves to me or maybe I just started to look at thing differently. The natural cycles of life are everywhere, one thing feeding off another. The seal is not the great white shark's victim any more than the anchovy is the seal's. They are all just playing a role in the big picture.

The realizations were everywhere and would just pop out at me. I was driving and pulled up to a long traffic light. Not paying attention to anything in particular, I looked at a tall weed by the side of the road. It was the kind that grows in the canyons around San Diego. As kids we used to walk by them, grab the stalk and slip our hands up to strip the seeds off. Then we would throw them at each other. The pointy end of the seeds would stick in your clothes and was hard to get out. It was only a few minute wait for the light but as I looked at that weed along the side of the road it was suddenly so beautiful that I started to cry out of joy. I could feel the presence of the Divine in it. The light changed, and as I drove down the street crying I remember thinking to myself, this is really getting out of hand.

I was becoming curious about the physical sensations on my head coupled with the drunken feeling that would not go away. It had been going on for the better part of a year at this point so I called a lifelong friend of mine who is a brain surgeon at Columbia. We have known each other since I was 16. Not only is the guy pretty bright but he is down-to-earth normal, not always the case for a genius. Until this point I had not told anyone what was going on. It was downright embarrassing. "I'm a man's man here! I fly helicopters, fire walk, own a yacht, run 100-mile races in the Sierras, drive Ferraris, fish for Marlin, break bricks with my bare hand and run with the bulls." Euphoria, seeing the synergies of all nature, inspired by a roadside weed to cry out of joy, bliss and all this other stuff is simply not done and certainly never talked about. I confided to him only about the physical sensations - feeling drunk, the clearly delineated energy around my head and the feeling as if someone was lightly touching my hair, moving it around. He explained that some tumors can create a drunken feeling but he had never run into my energy--around-the-head scenario.

I did not really want to tell him everything but at this point it became necessary on account of the possibility of the symptoms being caused by a tumor. I laid it out - forgiving, uncontrollable joy leading to crying, recognizing the synergies of life, knowing things before they happen, an absence of fear and worry, etc. His diagnosis - "You're in a really good place, I'd just enjoy it". He talked about certain guru's expressing these kinds of things. I let go of the concern that this was some weird medical condition.

Months passed, and the intense energy that I had been feeling in the crown of my head started to appear in my hands and feet as well. It felt like a drug or that my cells were changing at a molecular level. It was so intense that at first I worried it might be the onset of some neurological disease. Over a period of a year it crept up my arms and legs until it finally filled my whole body.

While experiencing these sensations, I was very mentally present, a sharp contrast to the way I had lived my entire life. Prior to these changes, I was mentally living everywhere but where I was at the moment. I lived in the past by thinking about resentments, past hurts, and longing for the good ol' days. I told everyone that the problem with going to Marymount Palos Verdes College is that you spend the rest of your adult life just wishing you could go back. When I was not in the past I lived in the future by fearing what could happen. I carried stressful anticipation, and the idea that I would only be happy after a specific event occurred, or some other desire was fulfilled. Most of us spend little or no time mentally in the present moment. Yet the best times in my life have come when I was living fully in the moment, not in the past or future. This is true for all people. Now I know for myself that this is where bliss lies. As you live mentally in the moment the issues of the past and future cannot exist. This presence is also the doorway to feeling unconditional love for yourself and for others.

Main new concepts I learned:

- Forgiving and letting go as I asked for a better divine connection caused a shift in my body.
- Life fits together perfectly; we are right on time even when it appears we are late.
- Everyone and everything is playing a critical role here on earth.
- The divine is in everything when I can see and feel that even an ordinary weed is beautiful beyond description.
- Everything is connected.
- Living in the moment is where bliss can be found.

"The opposite of love is fear
and all emotions are a derivative
of either love or fear."

———————————

"My answer to my fear was always
the same; make more money, get
better martial arts skills, isolate or
essentially get bigger and better and
no person or thing can touch me."

———————————

"The interesting thing is that when I
identified the fear at the root, and then let
it go, the corresponding emotion such as
anger or jealously just vanished instantly."

Chapter 7: Fear and Love

A friend casually asked me if I knew what the opposite of love was. I thought, what a stupid question. Of course I do. "It's hate," I replied. "Wrong," she said. "The opposite of love is fear and all emotions are a derivative of either love or fear." That got me thinking. I thought about Jim Johnson who I had hated. I told myself, "I ain't afraid of that guy! I'm a black belt damn-it! I don't have any fear!" I let the entire topic drift away.

I could not understand why I still had this feeling of hate for this person. I had forgiven him but I still felt this hate. Jim used to be a friend many years ago and also happened to be related, adopted by a distant uncle. Still, I found myself fed up with the very high level of manipulation. I was so tired of it that I just cut him out of my life. I would not respond to calls, e-mails and no longer involved him in any aspect of my life. I assumed he would get the message and just move on. We had business, friend and family connections so I did not want to make a big deal out of it. Having witnessed and experienced both his direct and third party manipulations, I believed it would just make a lot of trouble for me if I confronted him or called attention to this conflict. He held a great degree of influence over all my largest customers in our mutual business dealings, so it was complex.

When I quietly cut Jim out of my life his response was overwhelming. Emails consistently arrived with insults and accusations. Any chance encounter or business meeting became an opportunity to throw barbs at me. I reasoned that he would lose interest if I did not respond to any of his antagonisms so that is what I did. The problem only got worse. I found out from a friend that he had somehow developed a rapport with my stock broker and the broker had divulged a major loss of mine. Jim told my friend about it in excruciating detail. I told my accountant about this. It turns out Jim and I use the same one. My accountant said "ooops I have to tell you that he made it sound like you were best friends and so I told him some of your other financial data he asked about." I put my house up for sale and learned later that he was checking out the inside of the house and working with brokers feigning he was interested. I received e-mails from him with links to web cams pointing to exact locations where I was. I did not know what to do or which way to turn. It was all just so incredibly weird. It was unrelenting and I could fill volumes with additional events. I believed that if I went after Jim it would just turn him on even more. I thought silence was the best option.

Looking back from a broader perspective today, I realize that I was taught early on in my childhood to deal with weirdness from others by just trying to keep them calm and to avoid the lime light. I had a tremendous amount of fear growing up, and it had followed me right into adulthood. My answer to my fear was always the same; make more money, get better martial arts skills, isolate or essentially get bigger and better and no person or thing can touch me.

I finally started to talk to my family about the issues with Jim. They were shocked and wanted me to take legal action. I just wanted to forgive and let it all go. This approach had worked for me in dealing with my father but it wasn't working with Jim. Somehow I wasn't able to release the ill feelings by just forgiving. I wasn't releasing my hatred. Jim was here to teach an essential part of the only lesson we are here to learn. I just could not figure it out. They say that if you don't learn your lessons in life they just continue to reappear till you do. This one would not go away.

The lesson was finally forced upon me. I was out of the country when a family member passed away. She was a great woman, loved by all. After the funeral ended, in the church a mere few feet from the body of the deceased, Jim cornered one family member after another. Without any pleasantries he immediately began questioning them solely about me. "Where is he? What island? What hotel? I heard he got a boat, where is it? How big is it?" Nervous and caught off-guard, some members of my family answered his initial question before figuring out what was going on and then walking away. Jim took the data and moved to the next of kin, so to speak, repeating the information gathered, leveraging it to act like we were friends and to gather additional information. My family, with strong protective instincts, understood "what was up" and just walked away. When Jim got to my mother she became very nervous. She understood what Jim was trying to do but did not know how to politely get away. She became so nervous she answered his questions before being pulled away by other family members.

After I returned from overseas no one thought to tell me about what had happened. Life marched on and it was months before it came out but when it did I was enraged. That was it. I could not allow anyone to do that to my mother. I forgave but was still as angry as I've ever been. Then it came to me. The conversation that I discounted long ago. There are only two emotions - love and fear. While not afraid of this man physically, I definitely feared him damaging my business, my family relationships and my friendships. I feared the discomfort of knowing he could and would come at me from any or all of the above angles. I now clearly saw that my rage was not from a lack of forgiving but from a subtle derivative of fear. I let go of all fear of what might happen if I confronted him and assured him, in no uncertain terms, that I was ready to use legal or any other means to stop the behavior. I then confronted Jim, item by item, focused and forceful. He at first denied, then admitted, apologized and agreed to stop. In accepting anything that might come from confronting him, I was free.

I discovered that fear truly is the opposite of love. The concept that hate is really just fear started to make sense in my life. I am a man here, so I can't say "hey, you're scaring me!" Instead I got mad. It happened so fast and often that I had no time to recognize the anger-equals-fear equation. On top of that, I never wanted to admit that I was afraid of anything. Fear is a weakness and where I came from, any sign of weakness will be exploited by others. Anger is much more acceptable. It also means that I don't have to look at myself, because it's really someone else who is doing it to me. I guess anger almost acted as a tool to keep others in-check. Surely I had been on the other end of that many times. Fear turns to anger in a flash of a second, then anger turns to hate over time if you cannot find a way out or get away. Jealousy never felt like fear but when I looked at it from this new perspective I could see the fear. Whenever I had found myself jealous in my life I was really just in fear of losing a loved one. I started to look at my anger differently. When I would get cut off on the freeway and instantly flashed to anger I was not physically afraid of the person who did it but was experiencing a different manifestation of fear. I am afraid of wrecking my car. I am afraid being taken advantage of. I am afraid that he is going to cause me to hurt another person as I swerve and now I am going to be viewed as the jerk. The emotion of anger or some other derivative of fear happens so fast we don't even see the fear behind it. All we can see is the anger. Knowing all of this made life much easier. If I ever felt some not so pleasant feeling I started to ask myself, what are you afraid of? It took a bit of practice because I did not like to admit to myself that I was afraid of anything but I soon got the hang of it. Being stuck is also always fear, a fear of the future or of a loss of the past. The interesting thing is that when I identified the fear at the root, and then let it go, the corresponding emotion such as anger, jealousy or being stuck on something just vanished instantly. I started to hear conversations completely differently as I talked to others. If someone said they were mad I thought, "okay what is the fear here and let's talk about that." As soon as we found a way to let go of the fear, problem solved. This is also a great business tool once you understand. Have you noticed that people in positions of power who try to rule, manipulate or control others through fear are heavily invested in fear themselves? These people hold onto a lot of fear so they see it as the only real effective tool to influence others.

I've never really studied the Bible but I hear that the phrase "have no fear" appears in it 365 times. It's for good reason. As I surrendered my will to that of the Supreme Being, I began to understand that all happenings in my life are for a reason. With this realization, fear naturally subsided. As I kept my focus in the present, I found that fear did not follow me. Stress is just another derivative of fear. It happens when we project ourselves into the future and imagine what might happen. I spent most of my life in stress, the stress of what might happen when Dad gets home, the stress of what grade I might get in class, the stress of next month's bills, the stress of the boss and what he might do next, the stress of what the stock market might do next. The list goes on. Stress never stops. Resolve one issue and another takes its place. It's just fear. Fear feeds on itself and fear is hungry. Fear, whether in the form of stress or another derivative, needs its next feeding. The problem with fear is that it is magnetic. The old saying "your fears will find you" is true. Back test this for yourself in your own life. Have you ever had a big fear and then it happened?

The absence of fear makes room for love. Fear and love cannot occupy the same place at the same time. The derivatives of love are just as many as fear but are so much more fun. Joy, laughter, abundance, peace, truth, forgiveness are just a few examples. Each of these things feels good and actually makes you feel lighter. That is because the frequency they emit is higher, while fear and its derivatives emit lower frequencies.

Main new concepts I learned:

- Fear is the opposite of love.
- Fear and love do not occupy the same space at the same time.
- Only two emotions exist, love and fear. All other emotions are a derivative of those two emotions.
- Releasing the fear that is at the root of an anger, hate, jealousy, etc. will make it instantly go away.
- Surrender to divine will makes fear go away.
- Fear happens when we mentally live in the past or the future.
- Being stuck is fear.
- Fear is hungry and feeds on itself.
- Fear is magnetic, it draws to us the things we don't want.
- People that use fear to rule others are fearful.
- Letting go of fear and its derivatives allows room for love and its derivatives.
- Love and all its derivatives feel good.

"If you spot it, you got it."

_____

"You have only one of two choices.
Admit that the behavior is an
aspect of yourself that you do not
like or deny it and stay upset."

_____

"A great trick I accidentally learned
was to start to give to all others the
things that were lacking in my life."

Chapter 8: A Tough Pill to Swallow

It was summer again and I received an email from some old college buddies. They made plans to come out to the island and stay aboard the yacht. They just assumed it would be fine. I went along with it because I had not seen some of them for years. In fact, the last time I had talked to most of them, I was in a very different place, and I'm not just talking about my move 26 miles across the sea. It promised to be a very eventful trip.

Two of the seven that came arrived drunk and one of those was what I would call sloppy drunk. He caught a fish off the back deck and sprayed its blood everywhere, oblivious that he was tracking blood all over the place. He slapped one of our friends in the face and seemed intent on yelling, cussing, spilling and getting up in everyone's space. He had one of his friend's side-tie his boat to mine when I was not aboard. I was seconds from kicking him off, but he went to bed so I figured, "good enough - I will deal with it in the morning." I went to bed upset and awoke the same way. I talked to him and he said he was sorry. I thought that was the end of it all, but in a small town like Avalon, if you act up, it comes back to you quickly.

Riding to the shore alone in my dinghy for a cup of coffee and to get away for a moment, I was not halfway there before a friend with the Harbor Patrol pulled me over. "Hey Bill, who the hell do you have on board?" I explained it was just some old friends from college. "Well, tell them to stop with the cussing at people going by your boat, and the one that side-tied to you is trying to pull a fast one to get out of paying." He knew this wasn't the way I do things, so this behavior was a surprise to him. All I could say was that I was sorry, and reinforced this wasn't the way I rolled. On shore with my coffee, I ran into the van driver that takes me from town to the island airport. The trip takes a half hour each way, so we've spent a lot of time together and become friends. The day before the driver had transported the two friends who had arrived drunk from the airport to town, while I went back in my copter to bring more over. My friend the driver pulled me aside to say that my friends were cussing up a storm on the trip down to town, making racial slurs and yelling at girls out the window. He could not figure it out. "That's not Bill. Why would he be friends with the likes of these two?" Again, all I could say was that these were friends from my past, and I was sorry. It went on like this as I walked through town and encountered people who had met my "college buddies." By the time I got back to the yacht I just wanted everyone gone. I talked to them and things calmed down somewhat, but all I did was just tolerate them until the day passed and they left on schedule. After they left, from about town, more reports came in of other unpleasant incidents. I was upset and glad they were gone. I was not yet at the point of seeing the tremendous "thank you" gift they had left me.

A couple of days later, I told the story to my sister, explaining I was still upset about these supposed college buddies being so drunk and offensive. She became angry too, but all she could talk about was how mad she was that they came over and got the first class treatment, all this free stuff, major mooching. When I hung up the phone with my sister, I thought, that's weird. She's not upset about their drunken, offensive behavior but about their free ride. We had completely different reasons for being upset and her reasons seemed ridiculous to me. I did not care that they got a free ride. I love to share.

Later that day I heard the saying, "if you spot it, you got it." I played it out against the incident with my college buddies, but I didn't want to believe it. "No, not me. There is no way I'm like my drunk, abusive college buddies. I don't do that type of thing." I was mad to think that I was spotting something in them that was in me. I rejected the whole concept.

After I calmed down it hit me. Yep. I am like them. Not right now, but when I was 18 and 19 years old, I certainly was. I could see in them something that I did not like about myself. I certainly am not proud of my actions at that time of my life. On the other hand, my sister had never been drunk and abusive and so was not mad about it, she was mad about something else. I can almost still hear it on the school yard, calling someone a name. They would turn around and almost sing "takes one to know one." It was more truth than fiction. Look around. Don't you already know two people that hate each other yet are so similar, or two gangs, two countries, etc? If you find yourself angry at someone else, you may want to think about how you are like them, how you used to be like them or how your thoughts and/or actions carry the essence of what they do. It's pretty simple. If you are angry at a person, they are here to help by reflecting a part of you that you do not like back to you. The trick is to "man-up" or "woman-up" and admit it about yourself. If we don't like someone it's really some aspect of ourselves that is lighting up saying "look at me. I don't like this about myself." We have a hard time realizing this, but even when we do, we want to deny it. You know, denial is not just a river in Egypt! (If you didn't like that last line, maybe there's a bit of a punster hidden in you.)

Sometimes you have to do a bit of detective work. It might be that you don't emulate the exact action of the person you don't like but it's the underlying essence of that action. Maybe thieves really light you up, but when applying the "spot it, you've got it" principle, you say to yourself, "but I don't steal." Look closer, do you take the towel when you leave the hotel? Keep the incorrect change in your favor? When the boss sends you on an errand do you tell him it took so much time because of traffic but you went shopping? It's all an aspect of stealing, whether money, time, or whatever is not truly yours.

Be grateful to people you don't like. They are helping to show you what you need to let go of. You have only one of two choices. Admit that the behavior is an aspect of yourself that you do not like or deny it and stay upset. It's best to know it about yourself, to mentally thank the person providing this lesson and then to forgive yourself, letting it all go.

When they are coming at you with judgement, dishonesty, jealousy, anger, prejudice or something else that you don't like, look at your thoughts. Do you ever think these same things? You don't have to voice these negative thoughts for there to be energy behind them, and it doesn't even have to be related to the person that is directing them at you. If someone is coming after you with these types of negative energy, it's a sign that you are also engaging in this behavior. Do you hate when a rumor goes around about you but love gossip TV? Do you get into the reality drama TV shows? How's the drama in your life? Everything is related. As a gift it comes back to you to illustrate how it feels to be on the other side of the energy. Over and over this gift is telling you that if you want judgement, dishonesty, jealousy, attacks, prejudice or anger to stop coming at you, you need to stop doing it in other parts of your life. It might not be an obvious, exact correlation, but look for the essence of what people are directing at you.

The solution is easy. In your mind, thank whoever brought it to your attention. Apologize and ask the Supreme Being to take the entire category, for example judgement, away from you. Very soon you won't be "lit up" or made angry as easily, and people will stop coming after you.

The lessons in this chapter were a tough pill for me to swallow. It's not always easy to see something about yourself, especially when it comes in the form of behavior you don't like in others. Thank those people that make you aware and that awareness is a first step to making those uncomfortable, unwanted actions go away. This was another key in the eventual understanding of the only lesson we are here to learn.

Main new concepts I learned:

- If you spot it, you got it.
- Be grateful to people you don't like. They are here to reflect an aspect of yourself that you find undesirable.
- If someone is coming after you with some undesirable emotion or action, look to see if at some point you did it to them or someone else.
- Admit it is part of you, and ask the Supreme Being to take the entire category away.

"Most of us fail to realize that stress is nothing more than a thought. Stress itself is not physical - you can't bottle it."

———————————

"Next time you are alone and think a frightening, loving, vengeful, or funny thought, just notice what happens to your body."

Chapter 9: Stress, Love and Water: The Work of Doctor Masaru Emoto

Dr. Masuru Emoto's fascinating work with water has helped me to better understand the relationship between fear and love, and the impact that both negative and positive thoughts have on our physical and spiritual well-being.

Dr. Emoto takes a sample of water and exposes it to a specific word, picture or music. He may express something fear-based such as hate, blasphemy, disease or war. Or he will express something love-inspired such as hope, gratitude or harmony. He then freezes the water and photographs the resulting frozen crystals. Here are a few examples:

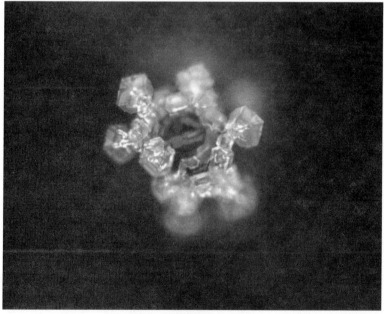

Despair

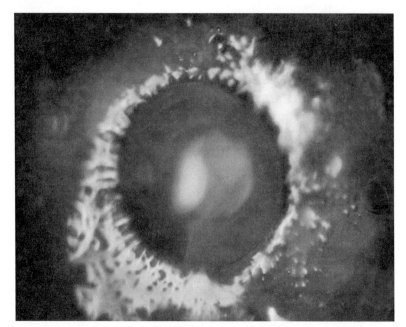

Do It

Let's Do It

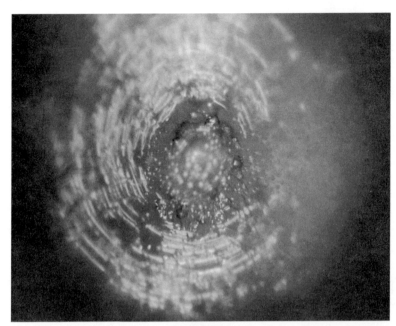

You Fool

Happiness

Love and Thanks

Hope

You are Beautiful

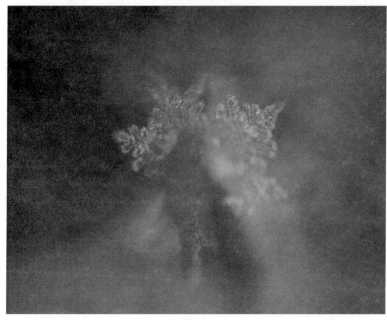

War

Harmony

As you can see from Dr. Emoto's photos, the water crystals exposed to a negative expression result in a much different image than those exposed to a positive one.

When you consider that our bodies are anywhere from 55 to 78 percent water, and you see the impact made on Dr. Emoto's crystals, you begin to understand the power that words, thoughts and feelings can have on our physical selves. If you're like me, it also matches your personal experience. When I used to worry about a potential future event I would become stressed. Sure as the sun rises in the east and sets in the west, this stress would lead to a very painful cold-sore developing on my lip. Each of us has experienced stress and we've developed our own physical manifestations of this stress. It could be an aching back, a sore throat, stomachache, sleep problem, digestive problem, a common cold, feeling tired or countless other symptoms.

Most of us fail to realize that stress is nothing more than a thought. Stress itself is not physical - you can't bottle it. At the same time, it can cause plenty of physical problems. Our thoughts, words and feelings affect us right down to the cellular level. You already know this by your life experience.

Without exception all of us harbor some hurt or resentment towards ourselves and others. It could be as subtle as "I don't like that person" or as overwhelming as "I hate that person with every cell in my body." It could even be against a part of the government or an institution. As we hold that thought we don't physically feel very good.

Next time you are alone and think a frightening, loving, vengeful, or funny thought, just notice what happens to your body. You will notice how just a thought turns into sweat, adrenaline, muscle tightness, butterflies, lightness, etc.

Dr. Emoto's work makes this clear. If speech can do this to water, and we are mostly water....well, you get the picture.

The Emoto Peace Project can be found at http://www.geocities.jp/emotoproject/

Main new concepts I learned:

- The human body is mostly water.
- Our entire body, down to the smallest cellular level, is affected by thought and feeling.
- Thought can cause us to feel physically wonderful or ill.
- Fear-based thoughts, negative judgements, etc. make us physically feel bad.
- Love-based thoughts, forgiveness, laughter, service, etc. make us physically feel good.

"As an altar boy, I was a bit of a rebel, ringing the bells way too long and way too loud."

_____

"To love another does not mean agreeing to let that person torture or harm you."

Chapter 10: Turn The Other Cheek

Raised a Catholic, I was sentenced to a lot of "Mass time" but served only out of obligation. As an altar boy, I was a bit of a rebel, ringing the bells way too long and way too loud. I would put too many coals and too much incense in the portable container that hung by a chain that I held for the priest. I think they must still be trying to clear that smoke out of the church! All the same I never missed a Sunday until I left home at age 18. As I heard the same Bible lessons over and over, my mind drifted away to anywhere but the present. One of the lessons - this whole "turn the cheek thing" was just not for me. Turn the cheek and get a beat down, that was my view. Better to stand up for yourself against those people out to get you. It was not until I met a very wise Catholic Nun years later that I learned the real lesson waiting for me. She happened to mention that the original Bible was written in Aramaic. When Jesus said, "turn the other cheek" it had a different meaning than it does today. In that place and time a person demonstrated dominance over a slave or supposed other lower class person by backhanding them. The right hand was used because the left hand was considered unclean. So here is the great part. If you, Mr. Lower Class Slave, were slapped and turned the other cheek, you forced your "slapper" into a tough decision. If he slaps you now with an open right hand, you then become his equal and you are free. If he slaps you with his unclean left hand, that is a crime and his punishment is to hand over all his possessions to you. Okay, now that works. That makes more sense. I never understood why Jesus would want to teach people to be victims. This explains it. He never did.

When I was growing up in the Seventies, I used to love this program called Kung Fu. Kwai Chang Caine, the star of the show would travel the old west, never looking for a problem but inevitably ending up in a number of fights (Hmm sounds familiar). Of course, the martial arts kick-ass session always came with a wise lesson at the end. I can't believe I still remember this lesson, told as a flashback to Caine's days as a student in the temple.

> Caine: Master, if a man tries to kill me with a stick, do I first kill him, or run?
> Master: Neither
> Caine: I don't understand.
> Master: You forgot your other option. You can take the stick away.

Though wise and a formidable fighter, Caine did not immediately see the other option available to him, just as I saw the "turn the other cheek" lesson through my own limited perspective. To love another does not mean agreeing to let that person torture or harm you. To allow that is to not love yourself.

Main new concepts I learned:

- The Supreme Being did not intend us to be victims.
- To love does not mean agreeing to allow harm.
- Allowing another to harm us is to not love ourselves.
- We have options.

"We believe that no one really sees inside our mind or knows what we are truly feeling. It's our little secret."

———————————

"We are all at that same gas station."

———————————

"You cannot hold enough resentment in your heart to make hurt caused by another go away."

Chapter 11: The Guy In The Gas Station

Life looks different to everyone and truly reflects back to us what we are thinking and feeling. We believe that no one really sees inside our mind or knows what we are truly feeling. "It's our little secret." To a certain extent, we are right, but the essence of our thoughts and feelings do come across whether we like it or not. Imagine this example; you pull into the gas station to fill up. You notice a guy a few pumps over and you can just feel the anger and hostility seething inside him. He is clean cut and dressed normally but you can just tell there's something about him. It's almost as if he just got out of the joint. There are no outward signs of hostility but it does not feel good. Your instant reaction:

"If this guy wants to roll up on me, the answer is not just no, but hell no!"

If he were to approach you, talking to him would certainly be uncomfortable. Even telling him the time would be uncomfortable. The interesting thing here is that this guy is only guilty of harboring resentments and anger. He has not so much looked in your direction but you are ready to resist him at the slightest contact. This guy's experience with you at the gas station is the same for him everywhere he goes. At the grocery store when he goes to buy a loaf of bread he finds people hostile to him even though he hasn't said a word. He goes to an interview with perfect qualifications but the person on the other side of the desk can feel it. On the surface nothing hostile is said and there is no outward discussion of his resentment but he can feel the interviewer's resistance and foresees the obvious outcome. It follows this guy everywhere. To him the world is a hostile place. People are mean although he has done nothing to them. It is not a misperception on his part that people are mean, because they are mean - to him.

The guy at the gas station feels he is just being realistic about his perception of the world. "I know how the world is. That is how things go." With a lack of any experience to the contrary, life for him continues as it has in the past. This is also our reality. Here's the thing. I was the guy at the gas station. You are the guy or girl at the gas station. We are all at that same gas station. How we are feeling is not the secret we think it is, and we can't hide it from the guy two pumps over, let alone our family, friends and others we encounter. If you feel disrespected, mistreated, avoided, and that you never get a break, you are correct. What you may not realize is that your experience is caused by something that seems completely unrelated to the event of the day. It's caused by not forgiving yourself, your parents, your family or others in your life for perceived misdeeds that happened either recently or long, long ago. You cannot hold enough resentment in your heart to make hurt caused by another go away. Only forgiveness can.

On the other side of the "feeling world" everyone has encountered someone that they just liked, felt at ease around, and had a certain positive energy to them. This person made you want to go out of your way to smile, talk to them or help them in some way. Now imagine this person as they go to the gas station, grocery store and an interview. Don't you think everyone else can also feel it? What do you think the experience they have today will be as they pump gas or buy a loaf of bread? Pretty positive. This guy's positive gas station experience is just as real as our first friend's bad experience.

Main new concepts I learned:

- Holding on to negative experiences from the past will bring to you daily negative experiences that seem completely unrelated.
- How we are feeling is not a secret to others.
- Others reflect back to us the very things we are feeling.
- People are treated better or worse based upon what they are thinking and feeling.

"He also saw that this angry friend he had known since he was 18 years old, yours truly, did not seem to get angry very much anymore. He had called to ask if what he was seeing in me was really true, and how could that be?"

———————————————

"I went to bed angry as could be. I got up the next morning still angry. I felt justified in my anger. After my second cup of coffee it hit me. I had a little 'conversation with self.'"

———————————————

"I came to the realization that these possessions seen as the source of all happiness were quickly turned into the source of pain."

Chapter 12: Letting Go

Before I began forgiving, fear disguised as anger played a major role in my life. Everyone around me knew it, even though I thought it was my little secret. I would flare up at this or that, thinking if I can get past this incident, or get that person out of my life, everything will be fine. After I started forgiving, I was overwhelmed with the joy and peace I felt. I did not even notice that I was no longer getting angry. No one was pushing my buttons. No one was backhanding me.

People have noticed the change in me. A longtime friend of mine spent a weekend on the yacht. In between fun on the water we started talking about fear, forgiveness, anger, irritations and a connection to the Divine. We went through a few meditations I had learned about releasing fear and forgiving the people on the forefront of your mind. He said the experience made him feel lighter, happier and free. After the weekend, he called to say that our work helped him to realize the countless opportunities he has to get angry every day, and when the guy in the car next to him cut him off, he feels justified in that anger. He also saw that this angry friend he had known since he was 18 years old, yours truly, did not seem to get angry very much anymore. He had called to ask if what he was seeing in me was really true, and how could that be?

I answered him that I now rarely get angry, and when I do, what used to take weeks to get over is now through in a matter of minutes or even seconds, without much effort. It was a timely question because I had experienced a great example. A new revelation had occurred to me just before his weekend visit.

This was the first summer I had returned to Avalon since I began forgiving myself and others. Moving the yacht to Catalina for the summer is a big undertaking so the day the move is complete is a pretty big deal. After my wife and I got our boat's mooring, we went to shore for dinner at my favorite Mexican restaurant. The following day a pilot was to deliver our helicopter, which would streamline transportation to the mainland when necessary, the final icing on the cake for enjoying the entire summer on the island. It was truly a dream come true. I felt so happy as the waiter set down my margarita. I raised it up to toast my bride, "we made it, to the start of summer!" Clink. No sooner than the very first drip of tangy flavor touched my lips then my wife piped up, "You know we are not staying here if I get pregnant." Immediately I got upset, very upset. My mind raced. I had worked my whole life to get to this place, from the time I was eight and picking up after dogs, to when I was 10 picking up unmentionables as janitor at the "pay by the hour" Rancho Rio Motel in Chula Vista. At 15, I was cleaning girls toilets at Hilltop Jr. High, etc., etc. As an adult, I had spent decades working 12-hour days in a job I hated. I had never taken a vacation yet had taken plenty of financial risks way beyond what was rational. All of those jobs and risks were aimed at actualizing the dream of owning a large yacht with luxuries to beat the band. My floating American dream offered all the comforts of home and then some. Millions were spent to make it wonderful and to top it all off, it was now paired to a brand new half a million dollar helicopter to get us anywhere we wanted to go off the island. It was even air-conditioned damn-it! In one fell swoop I was watching it all go away. I had spent the happiest moments of my life on the island and the thought of abandoning it all to stay in a one bedroom downtown condo my wife had purchased prior to our marriage just felt like being sent to prison. My beach house had been leased so there was no other option. We would definitely be in the downtown condo. I went to bed angry as could be. I got up the next morning still angry. I felt justified in my anger. After my second cup of coffee it hit me. I had a little "conversation with self."

"Okay, anger equals fear, so what are you afraid of?"

"Ah, hard to admit but I'm afraid of losing a lifestyle, change and being forced to sell my yacht and helicopter because we won't be using them."

I admitted this fear to myself but still felt mad and justified in feeling that way. Then I recalled that I had agreed to surrender to Divine will several months back.

"Alright. Here it goes. I am letting go of the fear of what is beyond. I am letting go of my will. As strange as it sounds to my logical mind, I know the greater good will be realized if we need to move back to the mainland and forgo the summer of my dreams. I let go of all fear."

It had been 12 hours since the first sip of that margarita, on the rocks with salt, facing a future with no yacht, no helicopter, no summer in Catalina, no actualizing my lifetime dream. Most of those 12 hours spent intensely angry or asleep. I let it all go. The emotional change for me was instantaneous. All the joy returned and I was happy. I let go of something that had been huge for me. At the same time I let go of all external things I thought would make me happy. Even though I had worked my whole life to obtain them, I came to the realization that these possessions seen as the source of all happiness were quickly turned into the source of pain. This helped me to understand my ego better and release attachments to all "stuff." I could still have and enjoy this stuff but was willing to let it go at the drop of the hat and not look back. If I had been unable to recognize the fear/anger connection and unable to release the fear I could have created a real miserable marriage. My friend loved the example because it was very real life, not a pie in the sky example. He had known me for so long, how hard I had worked, what I had worked for and how much it had meant to me. So to see me releasing it, really ready to walk away, feeling it and not just saying it, and ultimately experiencing joy made it real for him. It is our ability to release fear, to forgive, accept and to see the material world for what it is that removes resistance to a joyful life.

Main new concepts I learned:

- Admitting that your anger equals fear can be difficult in the moment.
- Releasing core fears immediately dissipates anger.
- The very things that give pleasure will eventually bring pain if I cling to them.
- The stuff of the material world is transient and temporary.
- Enjoy the material world in the moment for what it is.

"No, not even the thrill of skydiving could match the joy I've found today, but I sure gave it my best shot. In my twenties, jumping out of a plane was like crack cocaine for me."

———————————

"I always believed I was going to die at 28. I wonder if today is the day?"

———————————

"I woke up on the ground, tired and hot. I lifted my head up and said to myself "oh, I am so tired I am just going to nap for a moment," as I put my head back down and passed out."

———————————

"Knowing and feeling that these things are not the ultimate source of joy and bliss paradoxically lets me enjoy both joy, bliss and the pleasure of the material world just for what it is at the moment."

Chapter 13: Happiness Doesn't Fall From The Sky (or does it?)

Happiness has always been what I had - the relationship, possessions, wealth, status, physical pleasure and even health. Looking back at my life, I noticed one common denominator; each and every category of pleasure that at one time made me happy had later become a source of pain when it went away or morphed into something else. The categories of happiness revealed themselves as truly fleeting in my life, here one day and gone the next. And none of these things ever took me to the point of pure uncaused joy that I was now experiencing.

No, not even the thrill of skydiving could match the joy I've found today, but I sure gave it my best shot. In my twenties, jumping out of a plane was like crack cocaine for me. I used to love to jump, ecstatic over the experience of free-falling from 12,500 feet above the surface of the earth. It was wide-open adrenaline. I was a one man jet - rolls, flips and pointing my head straight down to reach maximum terminal velocity of over 220 miles per hour. I'd try all kinds of nutty stuff like jumping naked and surfing the wind with a boogie board. Many people do this today but back in the early 1980's it was unheard of. It was very what you might call "experimental "and I had a few close calls but was never really hurt. All that was about to change.

It was a sunny Saint Patrick's day as I headed to the Perris Valley, California airport. I had just turned 28 a few days prior and driving with the convertible top down, wind blowing through my hair (yes, at one point I had hair so just want you to know that) a thought went through my mind. "I always believed I was going to die at 28. I wonder if today is the day?" The thought vanished just as quickly as it came, like the wind through that beautiful mane of hair I had on my head. (Come on, you have to be laughing at that.) I was jumping from a new faster plane on this day because the usual one was down for maintenance. I was also using a new, extremely high-performance parachute with only a couple of jumps under my belt on it, but enough to know I loved it. That chute was like a rocket. I was the last guy out of the plane that day, jumping alone. As the plane passed over the point where I was supposed to jump, a group of jumpers going out together continually delayed their jump in the door, blocking me from jumping. "One, two, three, no, no, no. Okay, let's stage again, one, two, three, okay, lets stage again one, two, three no, no...." It was like some deranged Waltz of Delay at 12,500 feet. I started to scream at them "Get Out!" Finally they went and I blindly followed. You are supposed to wait three seconds in between jumps but I knew delaying any further would put me farther away from the airport.

I look down and see that I am miles away from the landing zone. I tuck my head down and pull my arms to my side. Talk about the wind blowing through your hair. More like through your entire being. I am screaming across the surface of the earth making progress back to where I should be landing. As I deploy my parachute I notice a barbed wire fence between me and where I should be. The angle of the fence is such that if I just perform a tight turn I will be on the correct side. I start making the turn. "Man, this new chute is cool." I am pulling "hard G's" as we say in the business, completely vertical in relationship to the chute. I am about three-quarters through the turn when I notice I have dropped a bunch of altitude and am hauling ass, as we also say in the business. I try to straighten out and flare to try to get control. The parachute collapses. I am still hundreds of feet up. I remember thinking "brace, you are going to go for a tumble, this is going to hurt."

I woke up on the ground, tired and hot. I lifted my head up and said to myself "oh, I am so tired I am just going to nap for a moment," as I put my head back down and passed out. When I woke up again it was hard to breath and I hurt all over, especially my leg and back. I reached back to pull my leg like you would if you had a charlie horse. My flesh moved in the direction I pulled it. I could feel the femur crack, and then again crack. "Damn," I thought, "I hate the hospital." I lost consciousness again. I have no idea how long I was in that field. I was far away from the airport and jumping alone. I awoke in the hospital, the doctors were asking all kinds of questions over and over. They asked and I gave them a number for my family. The doctor told me they were going to put my broken leg in traction, and that I might feel a little pressure on my leg. I laughed as I looked down and saw about four doctors holding the calf area of my leg while one of them had a hand-held, crank-operated drill with the bit pressed into my leg. It was so surreal. The doctor was like a kid using grandpa's old tool. He would get one or two turns of the crank done and then the crank would flop over. The doctors got the rod in through my shin so they could put the leg in traction, then attached and ran cables down to the end of the bed and put some weights on it to pull on my leg. The doctor calmly told me that I had a broken back, a broken chest, broken sinus and an exploded and spun leg. I was internally bleeding and had lost half my blood. They were not sure if I would make it, walk again or lose the leg.

Family arrived. Being St. Patrick's Day, Dad has celebrated it in the traditional custom. This caused issues in the small intensive care unit room when he managed to run into the weights a few times, causing them to yank on my leg and back. I screamed to anyone listening, "get him the hell out of here."

Looking at the hospital admission report several years later, it read that the patient is "combative" which may explain why I remember one of the doctors coming over to tell me, "You know Bill you are not the only patient in here." Understandably in a lot of pain from this intense accident, my reaction to the treatment during my stay was another reflection of what was really going on inside of me. The doctors, staff and some visitors reflected those feelings back to me. I just did not know or understand that yet.

So there it is. It all happened so fast. One minute it's thrills, fun, happiness and abundant health and the next it's gone, replaced with pain and depression. It took me over seven years to start to feel normal again.

Falling hundreds of feet from the sky did not immediately teach me about the transitory nature of happiness based on possessions and experiences. When I began to forgive and understand fear vs. love I started to realize that the threat of losing a happiness category or its actual loss would immediately send me into fear and all of its derivatives like anger, defensiveness, blame and a host of not-so-fun other feelings. It also pulled me right down out of the joy that I was now experiencing. I started to understand that the things that had formerly brought me happiness are to be enjoyed at the moment for what they are. They all have a life-cycle. Some will just end with my death but almost all will come and go before that. Almost everything has come and gone a few times for me now. I can enjoy each one of the things for what they are right here, right now. Knowing and feeling that these things are not the ultimate source of joy and bliss paradoxically lets me enjoy both joy, bliss and the pleasure of the material world just for what it is at the moment. This realization has filled me with a certain peace.

Main new concepts I learned:

- Pleasure is temporary.
- Joy and bliss are from the realm of love. Pleasure is from the physical realm.
- How others treat me and what happens to me is a reflection of how I feel inside.
- Clinging to the material world can pull me out of the joy and bliss space.
- If I see pleasure for what it is and enjoy it in the moment, I can experience joy and pleasure simultaneously.

"Our ability to feel love from the
Divine is relative to our ability to
love and accept ourselves."

———————————

"To love ourselves is essential. To accept
love from others and from ourselves
can be one of the hardest things we do.
I am pretty sure I am not alone in this."

———————————

"As we love ourselves we align with our
true nature, all the world responds and it
touches that same core part of others."

Chapter 14: You Are Love

Fresh from my most recent lesson about letting go, I meditated over a period of months, and began to feel the presence of the Divine. The love was so intense that I felt my body lighten up. It quite literally felt like I would float. My arms and legs would just start to lift off. I would do this every day and enjoyed the connection. One day it came to me as I walked on the beach. This love I feel in meditation, why does it have to be just then? I know what it feels like to have this connection and why can't it be like that all the time? I asked God for a message and quite clearly and immediately it came back, "You are love." It was intense. I started to cry out of joy. Good thing no one was around. The feeling of love filled my entire body. It was warm, it felt like I had been injected with morphine. I could feel it in my body and limbs and I am not talking metaphoric here. I could really feel it. It was euphoric. After a few days I started to work on keeping that feeling of love in me. If I ever slipped out I would remind myself to "get back and feel that love in your body." It was like feeling an energy inside of me. It reminded me of what it used to feel like when I would see my grandmother from New York. She loved me unconditionally and I could feel that in my body from her when I was a kid. At first I could hold this feeling of love in my body for just a little while. Later, I progressed to feeling the love almost constantly. It was like walking in the front door of Grandma's house in New York all the time.

A very critical piece of the puzzle was embedded in this very simple but profound event. In my life prior I did not like myself very much. Loving myself somehow almost seemed wrong. It was okay to love others but not myself so much. I knew growing up if you started talking about loving yourself that you would never hear the end of it, a wide open beat down would ensue. I am not sure how I got the idea that it was immoral in some way but that is how I felt. It was not till months later that it came to me. I need to love myself. I don't even know how it happened. I was just driving and I thought, "say to yourself, I love me". I started to say it in my mind over and over. It was like a turbo booster for all that love vibration that I already felt. The upper half of my head instantly had even more of the energy I described earlier and this feeling carried through my body.

I later understood that in not loving myself I had diminished my ability to feel love from the Supreme Being. Our ability to feel love from the Divine is relative to our ability to love and accept ourselves. To love ourselves is essential. To accept love from others and from ourselves can be one of the hardest things we do. I am pretty sure I am not alone in this. It seems much easier to love others, but as we deny love for ourselves it sets up an internal conflict. On the one hand we are love at our core, and the divine is love. Yet if we hate ourselves, continually carrying on negative conversations and self-judgements in our head, we are distancing ourselves from our core being, everything good, love in all its derivatives and the Divine. This distance sets up a cycle of hardship. Thoughts are magnetic and negative self-opinion will draw in others that will confirm it for you.

A good friend of mine named Al was having quite a few problems at a high paying new job. He had worked for this company in the past but when he returned he was promoted to a much higher position and this put him in a lot of fear. He was constantly attacked in this new role and forced to defend his job. The attacks were outright face-to-face and via e-mail.

I first attributed Al's plight to the corporate culture, but after talking to him, I realized we had to shift Al's feelings to get things to change for the better. Al was not only judgemental of others but very self-critical.

"Okay Al, here is what you do. Forgive yourself, stop judging others, stay in the present moment and feel the love in your body. Feel it for yourself. Stay in that state as you go about your work."

Al did all this and everything flipped. The boss of Al's boss wrote an unsolicited email to Al's boss, telling him how lucky the company was to have someone like Al working for them. People from other departments did the same. Al's head is spinning at this turnaround. His boss' head is also doing a 360. The co-worker who had been Al's primary attacker brought him in a gift card to say thank you for all Al's work.

The release of all fear is a natural side effect of maintaining the vibration of love. You will not need to fight it or tell yourself you are not afraid. As we love ourselves we align with our true nature, all the world responds and it touches that same core part of others. The next thing you know the attacks stop and gift cards show up!

Main new concepts I learned:

- I am love.
- You are love.
- Being in the moment, feeling love in my body is bliss.
- Feeling love for myself is appropriate.
- I feel God's love relative to the love I feel for myself.
- To the degree I do not love myself I set up an internal fundamental conflict. It manifests itself in a difficult life.
- Being in the moment and feeling love in our being changes others reactions towards us without a word being spoken
- As we feel love for ourselves we align with our true being and others as well.

"The ego is hungry for some identity, just pick one. It's also tricky because it can flip-flop instantly. It can encourage you to feel superior because of wealth one minute, and encourage that same superiority complex when you become 'enlightened'..."

"The guy in the mud hut may have a bigger ego than the lady driving the Rolls Royce."

"The ego's quest for identity tries to separate us from each other."

"We are all connected: you cannot have an enemy in this state."

Chapter 15: Ego as Big as a House

In my 30's, after not seeing Michelle for over a decade, I ran into her one night. It was the start of another go-around in our on-again, off-again relationship. A few weeks into the go-around, the subject my new solid gold Submariner Rolex watch came up. She had noticed it on the first night we had ran into each other and thought to herself, only a man with an ego as big as a house could wear a watch like that. I laughed, not sure if it was a compliment or an insult. So proud of the watch, I took it as a compliment.

At the time I really did not know much about the ego other than most people considered it a bad thing or tried to disguise it in some way. I thought a big ego meant you thought you were really great. I did not believe that I had much of an ego because I never thought of myself as "really great", but that was because I did not really understand the ego or its impact on my life. The ego sees itself as separate from others and often identifies with a group. It identifies you as a profession, man, woman, race, age, religion, low, middle or high social status, a certain level of education or lack of, sickly, healthy, activist, a list of accomplishments, member of a political party or anything for that matter that is us-against-them. The funny thing is, at all points of my life, I identified myself as all of the above, multiple categories at a time. I very much felt separate from all others. Even though everyone has one, the ego is a very tricky thing to understand. It's almost like it's an entity or person. It does not care what it identifies with - healthy or sick, rich or poor, proud of being a certain race or nationality, parent or child, skilled professional or blue collar worker, etc., etc., etc. The ego is hungry for some identity, just pick one. It's also tricky because it can flip-flop instantly. It can encourage you to feel superior because of wealth one minute, and encourage that same superiority complex when you become "enlightened," give up your material possessions, live in a mud hut, eat roots and shave your head. The ego does not care. The guy in the mud hut may have a bigger ego than the lady driving the Rolls Royce. None of it is who we really are. It is merely how we attempt to identify ourselves on earth. Our true identity is pure love.

My entire life had been caught up in all things ego. It came out as prejudice from an early age as I responded to the violence around me. Now, with this feeling of unconditional love inside me and a connectedness with others, I felt different inside. I felt differently about everyone and everything. Looking down at a watch that once meant so much to me, I imagined turning it over and taking off the back cover to discover the many beautiful, swirling, spinning wheels. Each one spins in its own time to its own rhythm. One wheel affects the next in perfect order. Each and every piece has a purpose. I do not understand the mechanisms and their relationships perfectly, but I know that if one element is absent or stops working, the whole watch fails. I see the watch as a different symbol now. It is our universe and those spinning wheels are us. We need each other and we are all interconnected. You can't have one part malfunction without all the other parts being affected.

The ego's quest for identity tries to separate us from each other. The worldwide silliness of prejudice came to me on a beach on the island of Bali in Indonesia. I ran into two distinct groups - the people that were from Bali and the people from Java, another neighboring Indonesian island. Everywhere I went, if anything went wrong or was missing the Balinese would say "Oh, yep that's the Javanese". I am sure if I went to Java they would say "Oh, yep that's the Balinese". This was all quite serious to them, just as it is to the English/Irish, Crips/Bloods, Jews/Arabs, North Korea/South Korea, Hell's Angels/Mongols, etc., etc. If I took one of the people from Bali and put them over in Ireland and/or England they would say," I don't get it. You look the same, act the same with very subtle differences, if any and I can't even tell you apart. On a worldwide basis, our ego drives us to believe that "we" are better than "them". "Who do they think they are? Oh, look at how they act. They are why we are all messed up." It goes on and on and on. I now see that everyone just looks at things differently. They have their own slant or perspective just as I do. Now as I encounter one of the "others" I look with my mind's eye at them, and ask to see their true nature. It's love, it's golden and cannot be seen by the veil that covers the naked eye, no different than me.

My ego was always on a judgment freight train, it's one of the reasons that I found so much conflict. As I judged others in the big and small things of life, it set off this cycle. Everyone else was judging me. Someone had told me long ago, "ya know, everyone is doing the very best they can all of the time.". When I first heard this I said to myself, "Aw bull *^#$!! You are telling me that when my father beat me, when all these girlfriends cheated, when people stole money from me or when Jim stalked me for years, they were all doing the very best they could at the time?" This was hard to believe. Come on now! Yet later, somehow things shifted again for me, and this "doing the best at the time" stuff made more sense as I looked at others from a new perspective. Each of the people who I believed had "wronged" me perhaps did not know how to respond to a situation. They may have been working from a diminished mental or emotional capacity. They may have simply viewed the situation from a different perspective. Perhaps they knew something was wrong but acted out of fear, lust or greed and obviously they did not overcome it. The bottom line is that they were in a certain place of their lives at that time. They were no different than me. They all had the same problem as me. The ego was in control and they saw us as separate. This realization allowed me to let go of my judgement of others. Everyone is on their own life journey. I accepted where others are at on the journey. When I see people making decisions or acting in a manner that I disagree with, it is natural for me judge them. Yet I know they are truly doing the very best they can with where they are at in their lives.

As I let go of judgments of others it made it easier to let go of self-judgment. Interestingly, as I let go of judgment of others, I noticed that people were much more accepting of me, just how I am. In every encounter with someone, I try to think something nice about them. I give them a compliment. I look at things from where they are at or send them a positive beam of light out of my heart. In focusing on a small gift for them it flips my thoughts away from judging.

This was put to the test as I entered the marine parts store I frequent. It's a "man's man" kind of place, no frills. Just parts and guys that know them. All the guys are old timers, been employed forever at the shop. I am waiting at the counter and I see a young guy in his 20's on the other side and I instantly feel his anger and arrogance coupled with my intuition that says this guy does not know the business. I think to myself, I hope I don't get that one. Welp, sure enough...can I help you? Damn. In a flash I thought no, don't judge, just send him love. I did it. I was right, he was an angry little guy, using it to cover up that he did not know how, who, what, where, etc. I knew this encounter had nothing to do with the generator parts that I needed. It was something else. He was here to help me with judgment. I kept the love flowing towards him and did not judge, just allowed him to be where he was although it was nothing more than a technical talk about parts, back orders, and other details, it somehow broke him down. The visit was much longer than normal but by the time I left he was smiling and giggling like a 12 year old girl. I almost choked up when I got out of the parking lot. I had seen beyond the surface, what the real reason was for all encounters. It has little to do with the surface and much to do with the underlying lesson that we were brought together to learn.

In every transaction I now saw in real-time two transactions going on. One of them for the ego and one for my true being. The one for my true being was a transaction or lesson if you will, of allowing the other to be, do or say what they want or don't want. Seeing the other's perspective or not. Passing judgement or not. Forgive or resent. Love or fear. The transaction for the ego was everything else. It became fascinating to go about my day in this new illumination. The transaction my ego was involved in seemed so petty and the one for my true being was fun, but covered over by a few levels of ego.

My ego, I guess just like everyone, had me playing too many roles. Blame was one of my ego's tricks. I had fertile ground in my sales job that I held for many years. When one salesman would steal another's deal out of their territory we called it poaching. Like everyone else I would blame the other sales person. It instantly put me in the position of "I am right and you are wrong." It made me better than the other or provided an opportunity to play the victim. Whew, these battles would keep you up nights. It instantly confirmed that we are separate and disconnected from each other. I discovered that the ego loves it, but it's just not much fun. Now I can see that in every event where I feel like blaming or when my expectations are not met, such as my moment at the marine store, it is just another opportunity to make the choice to learn the only lesson we are all here to learn.

Ego also plays the guilt card and it is very good at it. I was about eight years old when I got the idea to go two doors down and look in our neighbor's mailbox for the monthly delivery of Playboy. I must have heard from one of the other kids on the block that one of the older brother's got it in the mail. My heart pounded as I opened the box….oh boy, jackpot! It had a brown paper cover, very nondescript looking. I took the magazine and stuffed it under my shirt with my sweaty palms. I nervously walked to our house and around the side where I could not be seen. At my tender age I had never seen anything like this but boy was I curious. I liked girls from as early as I can remember. I recall catching a beating at about the age of four for laying on the kitchen floor trying to look up the babysitters skirt. Anyway, after my nervous viewing I stashed the Playboy in the bushes so I could come back later and review my ill-gotten gains.

That night I had one of the worst dreams of my life. I remember it in vivid detail to this day. I was in a desolate place, on a small hill, all dirt with no vegetation of any kind. It was hot and the wind was blowing the dust and dirt into the air. Papers were blowing around in the air as well. I looked up and I saw Jesus on the cross. The nails went through some paper and then through Jesus' hands and feet. As I got closer, I could see that the papers were actually pages out of the Playboy. I was overcome with guilt. I carried that guilt all my life. You are the first to hear about it. As an eight year old boy from a strict Irish-Catholic family, I believed that I really put Jesus on the cross and did that to him. Whew, guilt. Another ego trick. It has a purpose, for about two seconds, to signal us that we were off track and not to do that again. Anything more than that is useless suffering. If the Divine unconditionally loves and accepts me just as I am why am I not giving that to myself? My ego is the creator of this pain. It was another of the roadblocks to feeling the real you. You can experience this pain and beat yourself up or you can feel unbelievable bliss through letting it go and feeling the love that is already you at your core. You cannot have both.

By merely noticing my ego I was able to see it for what it is. It's impossible to escape labels while living in the world as we do our jobs, pursue our passions and live our lives. I just needed to learn that those labels are just labels, one of the ego's tricks. There are a lot of them - being offended, feeling superior, feeling inferior, wanting something and not accepting what is, and many more. We just need to know that the ego is not who we really are. As you enter into the state of feeling unconditional love, the ego's hold will naturally subside. We are all connected; you cannot have an enemy in this state.

Main new concepts I learned;

- The ego is tricky. It wants us to have an identity other than our true core nature, which is pure love and infinite.
- The ego sees us as separate. Our true nature is connected and necessary.
- Ego causes problems, from the interpersonal, to race, to institutions and governments.
- Ego's byproduct of negative judgement can be overcome by a focus on service or giving a gift with every interaction, such as a kind word, smile, positive thought or blessing.
- Everyone is doing the best they can.
- In every interaction we have two transactions, one for the ego and one for our true nature.
- As I stop judging others, they accept me as I am and lose fear of me.
- Just observing the ego will help to keep it in check.

"You would have thought I was at the Ritz-Carlton, every clerk was so nice to me."

"I forced myself back into the present moment, felt that love in my body and instantly the figurative spike was pulled from my head."

Chapter 16: Why Is Everyone Being So Nice To Me?

A remarkable thing started happening to me when I was able to maintain this feeling of love inside me. Everyone around me changed. The "known hostiles" suddenly wanted to talk to me, and would go out of their way to see me. Admirals, garbage men, billionaires, 7-11 clerks all just wanted to talk. People everywhere just smiled. I laughed after my latest visit to the California Department of Motor Vehicles, the infamous DMV. I stayed in the vibration and went to four different windows to get the job done. You would have thought I was at the Ritz-Carlton, every clerk was so nice. One after the next they just wanted to have a chit-chat. I took my test and failed but the DMV clerks took care of me and seemed to revel in my success.

> Clerk #1: "You failed. No problem, I just have to ask you a question, what does a red light mean?"
> Me: Ahhh stop?
> Clerk#1 Congratulations! You passed!
> Clerk#2: (from a previous window, now dropping by) "Did you pass?"
> Me: "Yes."
> Clerks #1, #2 and also #3 (cheering) YEA!
> Random Guy in DMV Line: "Did you pass?"
> Me: "Yes."
> Random Guy: "Alright. Way to go."
> Me (to myself): "What the heck? This is so surreal."

Now, Instead of asking where the parking place is I simply say that "I sure would like the one and only one right in front of the building." When it happened the first time I thought "Ah, no, that was just luck." After the fifth time I started to believe.

Ironically as I experienced this change, many friendships seem to dissolve. Nothing was said and no bad feelings came through but they just no longer called. This was the same for other dysfunctional relationships, nothing was said but they just seemed to go away. In the past this would have been grounds for great stress but it seemed natural and peaceful for me. I just let it be. New people showed up in my life, mostly of a higher frequency.

The DMV incident was followed by another one at a place also not associated with great joy, the dentist's office. A couple of cracked and failing crowns made a trip necessary, and when I made the appointment I was told to expect a bill of about $2,500. Mind you, this is the world's most expensive dentist. He's a professor and the dentist that other dentists prefer –the "dentist to the dentists" if you will. There's nothing free once you step in the office.

My concern was not just the cost but hoping that I could avoid a big "hack 'em up" session and fix things up on my initial visit, not the series of endless visits that can come with serious dental work. As I sat back in the dental chair with the light in my eyes, I decide to share this with my dentist that I lost my job a while back.

"Sure would be nice if you could just fix them today."

"I think we can bring this back and the other one too."

With no shot and an hour and fifteen minutes of work, the dentist is finished and my crowns are restored. As he is finishing up, I think to myself, "it sure would be nice if he didn't charge me anything." A few moments later, as I'm handing over my credit card to the receptionist, she says "You are all good. No charge today."

I was shocked. I went back to say thank you to the dentist and gave him a big hug. He made me stop because he said it was going to make him cry. It started to make me understand how deeply others can feel this vibration.

I went into a meeting with my partner to a group of known hostiles that we have had problems with since day one. Nothing is ever right. The truth of the matter is they just did not like me and have no problem making it known. I did not say anything to my partner on the way to the meeting but decided that I was just going to stay in the moment and keep the feeling of that unconditional love inside me, feel it in my body. In the meeting I stayed with this feeling and as usual my partner did most of the talking. It was strange, no barbs were thrown by the hostiles and they were actually laughing at points. I stuck to my usual topics, like the weather. In the middle of the meeting my attention wavered and I quickly slipped into the past. As I looked at the leader across the table, I thought of something they had done in the past, and began judging them. WHAMMO. All of a sudden someone ran a stake right into my brain just above my eye, or so it felt. It was so piercing and painful, I nearly put my head down on the table. The thought flashed, "what the heck is going on?" Instantly it came to me. "Go back. Go back. Go back." I forced myself back into the present moment, felt that love in my body and instantly the figurative spike was pulled from my head. I had no more pain. It happened amazingly fast. It was as if the Divine wanted to make the point very clear both on the up and down side. At the end of the meeting my partner left the meeting room for a moment, leaving me alone with the group. The leader beside me leaned over, looked me in the eye and said "I really enjoyed seeing you today. I am looking forward to seeing you again." "Me too," I said, and both he and I really meant it. I was in shock again as we drove away. I asked my partner, "how do you think it went today today?" "The best meeting with them ever" came the reply.

Main new concepts I learned:

- Maintaining the feeling of love in our being while focused on the present moment is extremely powerful.
- Others can feel the love in us.
- As people feel the love in you they act in a loving way back to you. No words necessary.
- Maintaining the feeling of love inside you will break down "known hostiles."
- Maintaining the feeling of love inside of you causes others in your proximity to be drawn to you in a good way. They become happy.

"All this peace and happiness surrounded me, seemingly without cause. I saw the synergies of everything happening just as it's supposed to."

———————————

"Happiness prior to the state of unconditional love is typically event-driven."

———————————

"I was filled with joy for no reason (or at least the reasons that I had previously thought were the causes of joy)."

Chapter 17: Uncaused Joy

A friend asked me, "What does it feel like?" I searched for the right word, initially could not describe it, and then blurted out, "like a multi-billionaire but only better." When I was growing up I used to ponder how it would feel to find a treasure of unimaginable proportions or to invent something like Microsoft Windows. I imagined the feeling would be so great that every day I would be happy. Ill feelings would just go away. I could have anything I wanted. There would not be a problem I could not make go away. Euphoria, a feeling of ease, lightness would all be mine and I could bring this feeling to others by buying stuff for them. That is how I believed it would feel to have that much money. I now know from experience of being a "thousandaire", millionaire and eventually a multi-millionaire, not to mention having a few billionaire friends, that more money does not equal more happiness. More money means just replacing the old problems with new ones while the ill feelings remain. Cross check this for yourself. At one time you were a "ten dollaraire," then a hunderedaire, thousandaire, millionaire, multi-millionaire etc. Once the temporary exhilaration of the latest purchase went away, how did you feel? I noticed after making the transition to a feeling of unconditional love that I felt euphoric. I was filled with joy for no reason (or at least the reasons that I had previously thought were the causes of joy). I felt a strange absence of all fear, a feeling that everything was fine and going to remain so no matter what came my way. All this peace and happiness surrounded me, seemingly without cause. I saw the synergies of everything happening just as it's supposed to. Events lost the emotional charge of good or bad. As I saw life from a new perspective, it all had a purpose.

Happiness prior to the state of unconditional love is typically event-driven. I just got a new skateboard, car, house, jet, degree, raise, skill, trip to Hawaii. I just won the case, got the recognition, overcame the obstacle, avoided a dreaded event, etc. Once you experience unconditional love and are actually feeling it in your body, you can get fired, lose the case, crash the car and you are still filled with a peace and joy beyond words. It is joy uncaused. It is yours and no external event can take it from you. This may feel weird at first.

"The house just burned to the ground and I feel at peace, still filled with joy. Something must be wrong with me."

It is difficult to explain to others who are distressed about an event happening to you, why you don't feel that way.

This is not about thought, it's about feeling. As you take on the feeling of love for yourself it will seem that everyone and everything around you has changed. The change is so sudden and dramatic that it's shocking. It certainly shocked me. For example, I landed our helicopter at the Catalina airport where my wife and I went inside the lounge to wait for the van to take us to town. We had just missed the previous van so had a bit of a wait ahead of us. A family was at the table next to us and the father was struggling to eat at the same time as his child of about 18 months old wiggled, wriggled, whined and worked to get off his dad's lap. It was to the point where people were turning and looking. I found it a bit amusing as I looked over too. The father looked up and said, you want him? I said yes and held out my arms. That kid wiggled off his father's lap and ran over to me. I picked him up and put him on my lap where he immediately laid his head down on my chest as I put my arms around him. He stayed that way for 15 minutes or so. Now and again he would raise his head up and just look at me and then put it right back down. My wife and the family all just stared with their mouths wide open. The parents explained that he has never gone to anyone. The mother simply could not believe it and the eight year old brother just kept looking and saying "what is going on?"

Previous to this, children were often repulsed by me and would actually cry when I approached or interacted with them. This event, waiting for a shuttle bus in Catalina, was still another sign post for me that all had changed.

Everyday now, this kind of stuff is happening to me. I have found that everyone and everything responds to the vibration of unconditional love. At the core of each of us is love, which is God. When we feel that love at the core and not just contemplate it, everything changes.

Main new concepts I learned:

- As we are filled with love we have no room for fear or it's derivatives.
- In the space of love the synergies of life reveal themselves.
- Seeing the synergies of life makes events lose the emotional charge of good or bad.
- Joy, peace and bliss are byproducts of love.
- Event-driven happiness or sadness is replaced with joy, peace and bliss the more that we live in the moment maintaining a feeling of love for ourselves and others.
- Children, adults and even animals lose fear of you as you cease judgement and maintain the vibration.

"All of a sudden it all made sense. Everything fit together. It was so obvious but I could not see it before."

———————————

"The problem for most of us is that we don't know that this is the lesson we are here to learn. No one has ever broken it down in quite that way for us before."

Chapter 18: Who Just Turned The Lights On?

I went to help a friend put up Christmas lights. She happens to be a Nun in her sixties, but you would never know it. She talks a lot about energy, quantum physics, thought and light. She is hands-down the most intelligent person I know and I've got a lot of friends that are Ivy Leaguers. We were casually talking as I was stringing up the lights. I don't remember how the subject came up but I told her about feeling this energy in my body of unconditional love, like when I would see my grandmother but even more so now. She said in her usual casual, confident, focused and precise way, "Well, you know that the only lesson we are here to learn is to love, no strings attached." Click, bam, what? Who just turned the lights on? All of a sudden it all made sense. Everything fit together. It was so obvious but I could not see it before. She left while I finished putting up the lights but later I found her to tell her I was done. "By the way, this lesson thing is what I call critical data. Do you tell people?" In the same way she always does, she said, "No, but if they ask me I will tell them." All I could do was laugh.

The problem for most of us is that we don't know that this is the lesson we are here to learn. No one has ever broken it down in quite that way for us before.

The more I thought back the more sense it made. All the people I read about and saw on TV with near death experiences coming back talking about experiencing unconditional love and acceptance from God. These people all experience a fundamental shift in their life after they came back and they start to treat others better. In effect they recognize that love is the only thing that really matters. All of the relationships I had over my life were better or worse depending upon how close I was in feeling unconditional love and acceptance for them. I felt better physically and emotionally as I started to love myself. It became obvious. Everyone was put here in my life to help me learn this lesson. Some were put here to play the bad guy role so I could learn about forgiveness, acceptance, judgement, etc. Some were in my life as examples of what it is like to unconditionally love. It also began to make more sense why it is the only lesson as reflected back to all the scriptures saying, "God is Love" across the world and time. The message I received on the beach that "you are love" and the feeling of it in my body. That same bliss state while meditating and feeling the presence of the Divine. It's in me and everyone else. I had simply forgotten this through life experience. In learning the lesson we are just simply remembering our core, the very essence of what we are.

Main new concepts I learned:

- The only lesson we are here to learn is to love, no strings attached.
- Learning the lesson is just a return to who we really are.

"One important piece of the puzzle is service...It's true. Love without service is not love. But it's important to understand that service is not the path to love....Service is actually a byproduct of feeling love."

———————————

"You may not decide to go to the streets of Calcutta to help the poor because it is not your calling but you will not be able to resist the urge to open a door for someone, say a kind word..."

Chapter 19: Now That The Lights Are On: Understanding Love

Scanning the TV stations I came across an old movie from the 1930's era, and heard one of the actors stay to the other "yes, we'll have a gay old time." I also remember that phrase in the theme song to the popular 1960's Flintstones cartoon series. It struck me that no one uses that phrase anymore, and if they did, it would mean something quite different than it did in the relatively near past. Would a teenager today have ever heard someone use that phrase in the context of the movie or cartoon? In the 1960's "book" meant to leave and 20 years before that it was just something you would read. When I see TV programs examining hieroglyphics on the pyramids there always seems to be some doubt about what those inscriptions really mean. Consider these recent examples and think of spiritual texts literally thousands of years old. They are converted from language to language to language with each translator interpreting things in their own way. Even with every translator's best of intentions, by the time the work gets into my hands, you can see how I might not quite understand what the very first guy, thousands of years ago, really meant to convey. I am pretty sure that the Supreme Being never sent a message to kill because of race, religion, sex or political beliefs. Many of the messages sent thousands of years ago have become distorted, so much so that it has pushed people away from religions that were designed to bring the original lesson to them. The funny thing is that the lesson is so simple. It is unconditional love. To reside in a state of unconditional love, and to really feel that love, captures the very essence of all the teachings.

Near death experiences provide a valuable clue to this power of unconditional love, while our increasingly connected world allows us to easily share and learn from those experiences. These stories help us understand what is really important. Many people come back and talk of an overwhelming sense of being unconditionally loved almost beyond their ability to verbalize. They are struck by the realization that we are all connected or actually one. All worries are vanquished; the only thing that seems to matter is the feeling of love. Many who have come back from near death describe an experience of re-living their life accompanied by a strong feeling of intense love and acceptance from the Supreme Being. They experience this love and observe their life not just from their own perspective, but also from the perspective of other parties in their life, especially people they have come into conflict with. They experience every conflict again, but this time as the other people they've encountered, including any physical and emotional pain resulting from that encounter. This happens because we are truly all one. You are the other person. You are the guy at the gas station. Some people are surprised when then realize what they did and did not do for their fellow men and women. Do unto others as you would have them do unto you. Love your brother as yourself. Not just idle chit chat.

People who come back talk about this incredible love and acceptance they feel from their Supreme Being, while continuing to judge themselves. I realized that this is what I have been doing here on earth. I judge myself and others, and in turn create my own punishment right here. In contrast, the less I judge, the more I let go, the closer I come to bliss. I create it all in either direction. Looking back, all punishments and rewards are my own doing. Each has its perfect place in the portrait of my life. Like a puzzle, I need to figure out where each piece goes, how perfectly it completes the other piece next to it how it helps complete the whole picture. Each piece helping to bring me closer to seeing the lesson, genius, masterpiece design of love with no strings attached.

One important piece of the puzzle is service. Everyone has heard the old saying "Love is not love till you give it away." It's true. Love without service is not love. But it's important to understand that service is not the path to love. Emulating Dudley Do-Right doesn't automatically get you on the love train. Service is actually a byproduct of feeling love. When you are in the state of unconditional love, helping others just feels so natural that the word service no longer even seems to fit. It becomes second nature to give a gift with every encounter you have with another. The gift can be as simple as a silent blessing, sending golden light from your heart to someone or quietly forgiving them. It can be letting something go, giving a compliment, or handing over a stick of gum. When we are not in the state of feeling unconditional love the actions of someone like Mother Theresa appear to us as suffering. For many of us it would be. To her it wasn't suffering, it was a life of joy. You may not decide to go to the streets of Calcutta to help the poor because that is not your calling but you will not be able to resist the urge to open a door for someone, say a kind word, express sincere gratitude for the service of others towards you, lend a hand with joy and ease, tip people who never get tips, and naturally engage in other acts of kindness. You will see the opportunities everywhere. Your thoughts, time, physical effort and money are natural ways to express service. It will not feel like drudgery, it is an expression of joy. If you find yourself doing service and it feels like drudgery, then you have slipped out of that love space. In every encounter humans have the tendency to judge the other person. Yet if we focus on giving the gift of service we eliminate judgement.

Main new concepts I learned:

- Meanings of words and phrases change over time. Ancient spiritual text can be confusing because of this. The essence of the teachings is unconditional love.
- Near death experiences show us that the most important thing is unconditional love and acceptance. We are one. What we do to others we do to ourselves. Our actions have a big impact.
- We create our own punishments and rewards right here on earth.
- Love without service is not love.
- Service is a byproduct of love.
- Service can be as simple as a positive thought, a forgiveness, a stick of gum or a wink and a smile.

"I saw a different path, and it was as simple as just letting go."

———————

"This state of living a life of love with no strings attached is not a super human achievement. It is our natural state. That is why everything contrary to it feels so bad and being in it feels so good."

———————

"In the presence of love, resentments go away, struggles cease, fear subsides and service is second nature."

Chapter 20: It's Simple

All of us have the ability to reach the same state of bliss. It's relatively easy to do when compared to the alternative. The amount of effort, energy and emotion that it takes for us to resent, judge, blame and argue far exceeds what is necessary to enter into this state of bliss. You cannot fight your way into this state. It is only achievable through letting go. Very simple. You don't have to read a book that tells you what it is by telling you what it is not. You don't have to read spiritual literature. You don't have to grasp a far out or lofty concept. You do not have to listen to a confusing lecture. You don't have to be a vegetarian or do Yoga. Mind you, there is nothing wrong with any of these things. You may find yourself drawn to one or all of them as they support you on your journey. They are simply not prerequisites.

I always felt that God was up there somewhere and maybe if you go to a cave in Tibet and meditate for 50 years or so you could experience that divine source. Surely that is one way to get there, but now I saw a different path, and it was as simple as just letting go.

We can wear a shirt with Namaste, Peace or One World on the front of it. We can perform yoga until we have the body of Adonis. We can read the Bible until we go blind. We can study, wear the robes of a monk or don the collar of a priest. We can eat nothing but leafy greens for every meal but we cannot hide from what we are really feeling. Look around you for the evidence. It is so easy to identify it in others just by looking at them and their life circumstance. Now look at your own life. Yes, this is a little harder to do and not so pretty to look at....but we are about to change all that!

Here's something to try. Picture yourself as a hot air balloon. Love is the hot air. The ballast or sand bags that are keeping you on the ground are fear, blame, resentments, judgments, ego identification, etc. As you drop the metaphoric ballast, you rise. You are light and free. As you allow this feeling of love in and give it to others in service, you ascend. The entire world is now viewed from a new and broader perspective. The more ballast you drop the higher you go with your love. With each bag you drop, everything in your life becomes easier.

This state of living a life of love with no strings attached is not a super human achievement. It is our natural state. That is why everything contrary to it feels so bad and being in it feels so good. Right now, picture in your mind someone that you really dislike. How does that feel? Okay, now go back in time and picture someone that you felt loved you unconditionally. Not so good on the down side but so nice on the upside, huh? It is all just that simple. You already know that your spirit is very light and your physical body is very dense, operating at a much lower frequency. Lower frequency thoughts such as regret and mistrust resonate much more intensely in the body. They can expand and take you over. Getting rid of the lower frequency makes room for more of the higher and it feels so damn good in the body to boot!

Across the millennium all of the great teachers such as Buddha, Jesus Christ, St. Francis and Mother Theresa have pointed to and lived lives of true unconditional love. They were all just humans, yet were remarkable for their willingness to live in a state of love. As a natural consequence of this unconditional love several things transpired - enlightenment, teachings and miracles.

It is that simple, it is the magic potion for all problems of every kind. If you are a hoarder it will just stop, it is no longer your focus. The material world ceases to affect you as it once did. Giving up a possession will be like pouring out a half a glass of water that someone left in the sink. It no longer hurts, even when letting go of your most prized possessions. It's very hard to be depressed when you are filled with love and joy uncaused.

Before I wrecked the yacht and started this chain of events, people would bark at me about this or that and immediately I would feel upset and bark back. It was so predictable. It was like a coo-coo clock, for every tick you'd get a tock. Over the course of time the barking at me diminished and as it did my desire to bark back slowly faded to the point of going away. People were not barking at me. As a matter a fact they were being very nice. A substantial change had occurred but it was so subtle that I had not really taken note. It became more consistent and obvious as time progressed. My feelings of frustration or anger were replaced by a feeling of compassion for the other person.

When I did slip out of this state, like the time I believed I was going to lose everything I had worked for, the reason for my "losing it" quickly became clear. I retreated back to identifying with my ego's version of who I am. At the same time I mentally dropped out of the moment, and started projecting myself into the future and fear.

It all seems so simple now. The closer I get to unconditional love or who I really am the more I feel joy-filled bliss and life goes easier. The farther away I get, the worse I feel, nothing makes sense and life gets hard. It's a gradient scale. On one end of the scale is fear, anger, hate, greed, living in the past or future, isolation and blame. As I moved to the other end, there was forgiveness, laughter, being present, joy, letting go of clinging to material possessions, the physical material world and seeing myself and others as infinite, unconditional love.

In the presence of love, resentments go away, struggles cease, fear subsides and service is second nature. If you take on, feel and become one with the feeling of love in your body you will automatically learn the only lesson that we are here to learn - to love with no strings attached.

Main new concepts I learned:

- To enter into this state of bliss one needs to forgive and let go. This takes much less effort than it takes to hold on to the negative feelings.
- Living in a state of unconditional love and acceptance is not a super human achievement.
- Learning the lesson is as simple as just letting go.
- Life gets harder the more one fears and easier the more one loves.

"I would often emotionally struggle with what I could do to help my siblings or mother when I saw them stuck in an abusive relationship with family, friends, lovers or in a business."

_____

"When I intervened, I hampered my siblings from learning the lesson that they had set up for themselves."

Chapter 21: Allow

Allowing others to just be where they are has become natural for me, a stark contrast to my life prior to the changes I went through. Not allowing others to do, say and be what they desire is another way my ego expresses itself, and I guess that applies to everyone's ego. I was the oldest boy and one of the oldest kids in a family of 12. This gave me a lot of opportunity to express who should be doing what and when. I would often emotionally struggle with what I could do to help my siblings or mother when I saw them stuck in an abusive relationship with family, friends and lovers or in a business. I would go aggressively on the attack against the person I perceived as the offender. It never really changed things that much other than making the offender back off and getting money returned, but my brother or sister would eventually find themselves right back in the same situation with someone else. I realized that whatever they were stuck on would just cause the same problem to come up again somewhere else.

The reason for the problem reoccurring is pretty simple. When I intervened, I hampered my siblings from learning the lesson that they had set up for themselves. So they created another situation to try to learn the lesson again. It's the subconscious making it happen. They usually don't even know they are doing it. For my part it would cause varying levels of irritation. I was tolerating. In tolerating, we resent or dislike the other but let them be how they are. In tolerating, I saw that everything has its limits and underlying it, I still did not feel good. It's when we allow, as opposed to simply tolerating, that we give up all prejudice, judgement and control. All are free.

I did not consciously try to tell myself that I had to start allowing people to be, do and say what they want. It just naturally happened. I gave to others the exact thing that I wanted for myself, freedom to be, say and do what I like. Everyone is on their own path. Everyone is here to assist you in learning the lesson of unconditional love. Being in a state of allowing is part of that. In allowing we permit others to learn the only lesson they are here to learn in their own way and time. As you give this freedom to others without any emotion behind it, you in turn become free. The obvious exception here is harm. Allowing another to harm you is not loving yourself or them for that matter.

Main new concepts I learned:

- Tolerance is hard, allowing is easy and makes me free.
- In allowing, others are free to learn the only lesson their own way.
- Give to others the exact thing you want for yourself - the freedom to be, say and do as they like.

———————————

"I needed each and every person,
especially the ones that I had issues with."

———————————

Chapter 22: Rearview Mirror

Think back over your lifetime 5, 10, 15, 20 years ago and consider what was going on in your life. Something happened that seemed tragic at that time; it might have seemed like the worst thing in the whole world. As you look at it today can you see why it had to happen? Did it lead to something great? Does it make sense why it had to go down like that? Life makes perfect sense as you look at it in the rear view mirror. The farther off the events are the more sense they make. The same principle is operating this very moment in your life; it's all happening for a reason.

As I look at my own life in the rear view mirror it has all become very clear. I needed to make and lose money, relationships, possessions, jobs, health and two unborn children to understand the impermanence of things and how the very thing that made me happy also made me sad with its loss. I needed my father to do the things he did, without him I would not have the experience of forgiving and loving someone who hurt me so. I needed each and every person, especially the people that I had issues with. I needed the ones that loved me unconditionally like my mother and grandmother to show the way. They all helped to give me the ultimate gift of discovering and feeling the only lesson we are here to learn. I love each and every one of them, no strings attached.

Main new concepts I learned:

- I needed everything, including every event and every person in my life.
- A look through life's rear view mirror makes understanding events easier.
- My rear view mirror works all the time. Whether it's looking back 30 minutes or 30 years, it makes no difference.

"We had to create a little
chaos to get a cookie."

_____

"I see all of us as both teachers
and students of each other."

Chapter 23: A Shift in Perspective

My feelings changed about everyone and everything in the years after the yacht wreck. I experienced a fundamental shift in perspective as I realized that trillions of events brought me to this very moment. My parents had to meet, and of course my grandparents, great-grandparents, great-great grandparents before them. Millions of events in each of these lives, millions of events in my life to bring this very moment to me. I realize this very moment is a gift. Every person, place, event and thing is in my life right here and now on purpose. The big and small challenges before me are for a reason. They have been brought forward through all time to reach me at this very moment, all to support learning the only lesson we are here to learn.

I realize that we are all eternal beings; our bodies pass away but our being or spirit lives on. Death is natural, we all do it, but it no longer appears to me as the end.

I thought about how I used to make chocolate chip cookies with my sister when we were growing up. It was fun and only half the dough would make it into the oven because we would eat it raw. We even made the recipe backward one time just to see what would happen. (Word of warning - don't try this at home.) The "cookies" did not come out so good, but we ate them anyway. Even as children, we knew one thing that would not work if you want chocolate chip cookies. You cannot get out the flat sheet, crack two eggs on it, pour on flour, vanilla, salt, baking soda, a bag of chocolate chips and just throw it in the oven. We knew that we would just have a messy conglomeration of two fried eggs, melted chocolate, and worse. We had to create a little chaos to get a cookie. We had to crack eggs, put everything in a bowl and beat it until our little arms got sore. I realized that it is the same for all of life big and small. Chaos precedes growth and change. Having a child is a perfect expression of this. Chaos precedes the birth of your beautiful child. The chaos of my life was an essential part of the growth and change. This principle is true, not just for humans, but for all of nature, earth and the universe.

Understanding that the only lesson we are here to learn is to love with no strings attached gave me a whole new perspective of all of life's events. I see each of us as both teachers and students of each other. Whether we know it or not, we are all assisting each other on the path to learn the only lesson we are here to learn. All life's hardship leads us to this lesson. Events that previously brought about great fear now appear natural.

The fear-based tone of the nightly news now seems so silly to me. It is the opposite of love, if you buy into the "we're all going to die" and "the market is going to crash" mentality that draws viewers. Fear is hungry and the news feeds it. While I feel empathy for the real suffering that goes on in the world, I've come to accept that everything is meant to be, a hard lesson for all of us to learn. Grief is a complex process. I find a comfort and peace in knowing we are all eternal. I am mostly comforted in knowing that those who have passed are experiencing an all-enveloping unconditional love, light and acceptance beyond any human's ability to put into words. I am so grateful for the role that these people have played in my life, teaching me whatever part of the only lesson they were here to teach me. When these people pass away, I understand they are just in a different dimension, not the end. I do experience an intense energy drain like the times we have lost our unborn children. Sometimes, when a loved one passes I cry, but it is different than it used to be. It is a cry that releases joy. I see the talk shows on TV and they look and sound so different now. I see each person given an opportunity to forgive themselves and others. In some cases I then see love appearing and when it happens, it always makes me smile.

Main new concepts I learned:

- Everyone is in our lives on purpose. Many events put us all together right here, right now, to work on the only lesson we are here to learn.
- We are all eternal.
- We all go to the light and experience unconditional love and acceptance after death.
- Chaos precedes growth and change.
- Each of us is both teacher and student.
- All events support us in learning the only lesson.

_____

"Your cue to where you are at in learning the lesson is how you are feeling."

_____

Chapter 24: The Lesson

The only lesson we are here to learn is to love, no strings attached. All of us, with a few exceptions, are here on earth because we have not quite got it yet. Your family, friends and everyone you have ever met were put here for you to help you figure out this lesson. Be grateful for each and every one. The people that are the most difficult to love with no strings attached hold this lesson most intensely for us. Do not create resistance for yourself to the lesson by playing "what if" games in your mind. If you stick to the actual people and events in your life, it will be easier. Accepting self-love and love from others is key. Your cue to where you are at in learning the lesson is how you are feeling. If you are angry, irritated, annoyed, attacking, defending or experiencing the myriad of not so pleasant feelings, that is your cue that you need to make the decision to love and let go. If you have anyone in your past that keeps coming up in your thoughts and not in a positive way, they are here to help you with the only lesson you are here to learn. Ask yourself, what part of the lesson is this person here to teach me? Is it to allow, release fear, forgive or to show you that you are denying self-love? The method to learning this lesson is like concentric circles with you at the center, then family, spouse/mate, co-workers, neighbors, customers, etc. In the outer rings are the people on the other side of the world you have not met yet. In every relationship or contact with another, you are the teacher, student, or both teacher and student of the one lesson. The most important people to work with will be those closest to you both figuratively and literally. It is best to start at the center. As you make the decision to release fear, forgive and love (this includes yourself), you will experience life here on earth as it meant to be. To view ourselves and others with unconditional love and acceptance is to see through the eyes of God.

The lesson I learned:

- Love, no strings attached.
- Accept love from yourself and others.
- "What if" mind games create resistance.
- The lesson is learned through the people and events closest to you.
- The cue to where we are in learning the lesson is how we feel.
- Ask "what is this person or event here to teach me?"

Summary

Ask yourself in each contact or event, what was this person or event here to teach me? Underlying every encounter or incident in our lives lays one or more of the few basics that require release to support you in the only lesson.

- Forgive yourself and others.
- Release fear and all its derivatives.
- Allow others to be without judgement.
- Release clinging to stuff.
- Release in you the upsetting aspect of yourself that you see in others.
- Release resistance to allowing the giving and receiving of love.
- Release resistance to whatever "is" at the moment.
- Release the ego through observing it.

You are creative. You will find your own path to this end. What works for one person does not mean it will work for everyone. You can do this your own way. As a friend of mine said "it's all just different flavors, chicken teriyaki, baked chicken or barbecue chicken. It's all chicken, you can have it any flavor you like." While this book tells some of my experiences, you obviously will have your own and some of them might be much more shocking then anything I have described here. You may not experience the drunk feeling and energy I described but it does not mean you didn't get it. Don't get stuck on "I'm not feeling that type of energy on my head or I don't seem to have intuition that helps me find things." Everyone has natural intuitive abilities. Some will not have visions in the mind's eye but will clearly be able to feel something in the pit of their stomach, to smell things others can't, to hear advice as clear as a bell that no one else does or to just get flashes of knowing.

Many people have had the ability all their lives and assume that "doesn't everyone feel something in the pit of the stomach?" No they don't, and it's your gift. In any event, all of these gifts are just a side show. The main event is to learn one thing, to love with no strings attached. Do what works for you to arrive at that end. Know that is why you are here. Know that is why everyone else is here. Know that every moment of your life has been in support of you learning the lesson - the bitter, the sweet and the seemingly irrelevant. Every day we make many choices. At first you may have to think about letting go of the strings that you attach to your love. As you maintain the feeling of love inside of you more consistently, the choice of acting with unconditional love towards yourself and others becomes automatic. It is your true nature.

The more you live in the moment with this love vibration, really feeling it in your body for yourself and then others, all will become clear. Feeling the love in you is many times more important than thinking about it. Being of service to all is a natural and important part of your life but feels nothing like it did before. People, children, strangers and even animals will lose their fear of you. They respond to you with playfulness, kindness, love and joy. They want to be around you and talk, just about anything. Your intuition flowers in its own way. You notice an absence of fear and stress as a new feeling of "everything is going to be just fine" arises. Disrespect for yourself and others melts away. To hurt another becomes impossible. Judgments are replaced by understanding and compassion. The speed of your ability to manifest your desires increases until it becomes instantaneous. You may also notice an irony. Here you have tapped into the ultimate abundance but the desires you once felt for this or that material possession seem to have just gone away. You still appreciate them but the clinging to them has vanished. You can live in luxury villa or a mud hut, you feel no judgment about it and going from one to the other in either direction is no big deal. The seeming random events of life look very purposeful. Physical pain diminishes as health abounds. Happiness, bliss and joy are uncaused by all exterior events and these events cannot take your feeling away. The material world has lost its power over you. You are one, you are love itself.

Afterward: Do it Yourself

If you just perform the following meditation, I feel you can instantaneously reach a state of bliss, although for me it was a process. If you follow the directions you will experience peace, bliss and an almost magical existence. The balance of your life here on earth will be beyond all of your expectations.

So here it is…the short cut. No need to sit 50 years in a cave in Tibet.

1. Find a comfortable quite place to sit, relax and close your eyes
2. Breath
3. Be in the moment; no thoughts of the past or the future. Be right here, right now.
4. Give yourself permission to forgive yourself and all others. Let it all go, right here, right now.
5. Give yourself permission to feel love.
6. Imagine a person that you have felt unconditional love from. See that person in front of you. If you have never experienced unconditional love from anyone in your life, imagine the white light described by people who have had a near death experience. Feel that beautiful white light as it is surrounding you. You are overwhelmed with how loving and accepting it is. Feel this love in every cell of your body.
7. Ask that your true nature be revealed to you. Ask Buddha, Jesus, Allah, Mary the Virgin Mother, God, Angels or Saints for help. You are love.
8. Repeat, I love me. Feel it. Repeat, I love and accept my life. Feel it. Repeat ,I love and accept everyone. Feel it.
9. Remember how this feels and take it wherever you daily life goes. Be in this present state, in the moment while

feeling that vibration of love inside of you. Feel it for yourself and for all others. The secret is to feel that love in every cell of your body. You are already love. You are just removing the roadblocks to feeling it.

The biggest change of your entire life is about to happen.

Bibliography

A New Earth: Awaken to your life purpose by Echart Tolle Published by Penguin Group 2005

The Angel Bible by Hazel Raven Published by Sterling Publishing Co., Inc 2006

As a Man Thinketh by James Allen Published by Fall River Press 1992

Ask your Angels by Alma Daniel, Timothy Whllie and Andrew Ramer Published by Ballantine Books a division of The Random House Publishing Group 1992

Basic Psychic Development by John Friedlander & Gloria Hemsher Published by Samuel Weiser, Inc. an Imprint of Red Wheel/ Weiser, LLC. 1999

The Chakra Bible by Patricia Mercier Published by Godsfield Press a Division of Octopus Publishing Group, Ltd. 2007

Getting in the Gap by Dr. Wayne W. Dyer Published by Hay House, Inc 2003

Hands Of Light by Barbara Ann Brennan, Illustrated by Jos. A. Smith Published by Bantam Books a division of Random House, Inc. 1988

How to Hear the Voice of God by Susan Shumsky, DD Published by New Page Books a Division of The Career Press, Inc. 2008

Illusions by Richard Bach Published by Dell Publishing a division of Random House, Inc. 1977

Inner Peace Meditation CD by Sr. Joan Marie Sasse, OSB. Published by Desert Art Shop 2009

Intuitive Insights. Vessa Rinehart, CEO. www.MyIntuition.net

Knowing Your Intuitive Mind by Dale Olson Published by Crystalline Publications 1990

Opening the Third Eye by Vessa Rinehart-Phillips Published by Personal Transformation Press

Practical Woo Woo. Nancy Pabers, CEO. www.practicalwoowoo.com

The Power of Intention by Dr. Wayne W. Dyer Published by Hay House 2004

The Power of Now by Echart Tolle Published by Namaste Publishing 1997

Practical ESP by Carol Ann Liaros Published by PSI Search Publications 1985

The Psychic Pathway by Sonia Choquette Published by Three Rivers Press 1994

Law of Attraction by Michael J. Losier Published by Michael J. Losier 2006

Life and Teaching of the Masters of the Far East by Baird T. Spalding Published by Devorss & Company 1964

Life After Life by Dr. Raymond Moody. VHS 1992

Mutant Message Down Under by Marlo Morgan Published by Harper Collins Publishers 1994

Quantum Healing by Deepak Chopra Published by Bantam Books 1989

Return of the Bird Tribes by Ken Carey Published by HarperOn a Division of HarperCollins Publishers

The Sanctifier by Archbishop Luis M. Martinez Published by Pauline Books & Media 2003

The Secret by Rhonda Byrne Published by Beyond Words a Division of Simon & Schuster, Inc. 2006

Spirit Guides & Angel Guardians by Richard Webster Published by Llewellyn Heal Your Body by Louise L. Hay Published by Hay House, Inc. 1982

Trust Your Vibes by Sonia Choquette Published by Hay House 2004

The Way of the Shaman by Michael Harner Published by HarperCollins 1990

The Way of Zen by Alan Watts Published by Vintage Books a Division of Random House 1989

You Can Heal Yourself by Louise L. Hay Published by Hay House 1999

You are Psychic! by Peter Jr. Sanders Published by The Random House Ballantine Publishing Group 1989

Please visit us at www.theonlylesson.com to keep informed of our upcoming new book releases.